WHAT WOULD BRIAN BOITANO MAKE?

WHAT WOULD BRIAN BOITANO MAKE?

FRESH AND FUN RECIPES FOR SHARING WITH FAMILY AND FRIENDS

BRIAN BOITANO

PHOTOGRAPHS BY RINA JORDAN

LYONS PRESS
Guilford, Connecticut

An imprint of Globe Pequot Press

Lyons Press is an imprint of Globe Pequot Press.

What Would Brian Boitano Make?® is a registered trademark owned by Brian Boitano.

Photographs by Rina Jordan except those on pages v, 7, 23-24, 26, 31, 53, 63, 70, 82–83, 101, 104, 119, 122, 134, 145, 153, 174, 179, 186, 197, 208, and 215 supplied by Brian Boitano, the photo on page xiii by Amy Neunsinger, the photos on pages 96–97 courtesy of Dino Ricci, and the photos on pages 93 and 190 licensed by Shutterstock.com.

Project editor: Tracee Williams
Text design and layout: Nancy Freeborn
Food Stylist: Malina Lopez
Photo Assistant: Jessica Yager
Food Styling Assistants: James Dean, Jessica Baxter, and Lacey Morris

Library of Congress Cataloging-in-Publication Data is available on file.

ISBN 978-0-7627-8292-5

Printed in the United States of America

10 9 8 7 6 5 4 3 2 1

FOR MOM, DAD, AND AUNT TREE

CONTENTS

FOREWORD BY GIADA DE LAURENTIIS

To say Brian Boitano is a trend setter would be an understatement. He has a list a mile long of "firsts"—first American to land a triple axel, first to attempt a quadruple jump in competition, first male skater to be featured on the cover of *Sports Illustrated* . . . but my favorite first of Brian's has to be his first cookbook! Taking a spin from his hit series *What Would Brian Boitano Make?* on the Food Network and Cooking Channel, Brian has put together a perfect collection of recipes, sure to inspire everything from a chic cocktail party to a weeknight family dinner. In other words, in perfect Brian fashion, there is something for everyone!

Brian and I share a few things in common. Our passion for cooking is rooted in our Italian heritage, but a lot of our inspiration blooms from traveling around the world and being exposed to so many different cultures and worldly flavors. It's so much fun to bring that flavor home, turn it into a perfect party appetizer, and share it!

When Brian appeared on my show, *Giada at Home*, he let me in on the secret of his cookbook in the works. And I admit that I was curious to see what Brian Boitano would make. I am going to go out on a limb and say I think Brian has another gold here. The recipes are accessible, healthy, and a great addition to anyone's kitchen, especially those who love to entertain! The Crab-and-Avocado Crostini, perfectly paired with the Blood Orange Mojitos—yummy. You've got instant party perfection!

Like I always say, keep your friends close and your friends who can cook closer! From the ice on the rink to the ice in my drink, Brian never ceases to entertain me, and I will keep him and his cookbook close for a long, long time. Perfect 6!

XOXO,
Giada

INTRODUCTION

I really like entertaining. Maybe that's why I was attracted to both my passions, cooking and skating. Both build on a basic structure of skills, knowledge and rules, and have interesting layers on top of that foundation. Skating has your performance, costume, and the music; while cooking has flavor, texture, and appearance. In both cases, those layers are chances to crank up your creativity. It's kind of amazing where passion can lead you. My love for figure skating took me around the world and to the top of an Olympic medal podium. I never thought of it as work because passion has a way of making things—even 5:00 a.m. workouts, in a dark, refrigerated skating rink—seem exciting, fun, and full of potential. There's a certain type of thrill and deep satisfaction in developing new skills and constantly improving.

Nowadays, I find that same fulfillment in all things cooking and entertaining.

It might be because the cooking gene is a dialed-in part of my DNA. I come from a big Italian family and, as with most big Italian families, great food is pretty much always front and center. It doesn't matter if it's a wedding, a funeral, or a favorite holiday; delicious, filling food is a key part of the event. As a matter of fact, some of my favorite food memories revolve around family gatherings. My great-aunt Tree had a cabin that we called "The Shack." It sits on a bluff overlooking the Pacific Ocean, and as far back as I can remember, we'd regularly gather there as a family. Aunt Tree put out amazing spreads that introduced me to new and exotic foods. Smoked oysters? Check. Cactus in adobo sauce? You bet. A medley of exotic chocolates? Her rocky road was everybody's favorite and she served it by the bushel. She made the idea of trying new foods seem like an adventure. And it wasn't just the food. Meals at Aunt Tree's Shack meant casual daylong affairs of eating, hanging out with people you love, and then eating some more. Those days marked the beginning of my fascination with entertaining.

In a funny way, my career probably has almost as much to do with my passion for food as my family does. Compete as an athlete on the international level and you're forever watching what you eat. I've been on more restrictive diets than I can count (I can't eat beets to this day—don't ask). As a young skater in training I would watch fast food commercials on TV and dream of the day I could claim a Whopper or a bucket of KFC for my very own, guilt free.

Fast-forward to about the time I turned twenty-five, when I began cooking for myself and my friends. It was at the end of 12 months of nonstop traveling in the year after I won the Olympic gold medal in figure skating. There's nothing like a hectic world tour to make you want to be "home" in every sense of the word, and for me that was San Francisco. I was lucky enough to find a great house in my favorite neighborhood. I unpacked, set up my kitchen, and settled in. I was home!

In my down time, I was hanging out with a group of six close friends who, like me, had big appetites and loved good food. I was the only one who owned a house—so my kitchen became the designated gathering spot. It didn't take long for us to fall into a regular routine of cooking dinner together almost every night. One person would make the main course, someone else would bring the wine, and another person would handle dessert. We'd decide on the fly what we were going to cook. One night it might be grilled salmon with saffron risotto; the next night it might be braised pork shoulder with green beans amandine (I'm getting hungry just writing this). No matter what it was, preparing the meal was every bit as social and fun as eating it. Taking what I'd learned from Aunt Tree about mixing people and interesting food, those first meals were spontaneous and casual, and some of my favorite meals ever.

Over the next twenty years I traveled all over the world for skating, and the more I traveled, the more it influenced my cooking. I was introduced to all kinds of cuisine, from French to Spanish to Russian, and all kinds of dishes, from sushi to hot and spicy New Orleans fare. But I always looked forward to coming home and sharing my newest discoveries with my friends and family. I began experimenting more in the kitchen, and it evolved into the process that I still use today, even when I'm cooking for myself. If I'm not on the road, I head to the local farmers' market, butcher, or seafood shop and look for interesting ingredients that I can mix and match in new flavor combinations. Today it might be mustard greens that hook my imagination; tomorrow it might be goat chops.

After shopping, I get down to it chopping and mixing. Sometimes I'll work late into the night, all alone with no distractions, trying out variations and perfecting a recipe. I love the creativity of cooking, the anticipation, and the smells. But my favorite part is when it all comes together and it's time to plate the food. You can just see it when the dish turns out the way you want it to, even before you taste it. When I'm satisfied with the recipe, I write it down in a journal alongside a picture of the finished dish. Many of the recipes in this book come from that journal.

My love of food and entertaining eventually led to my Food Network show, *What Would Brian Boitano Make?* That has, in turn, led to my writing this cookbook, *What Would Brian Boitano Make?* How about that, they have the same name . . . go figure.

So here it is—the recipes in this cookbook represent an eclectic mix of tastes and influences from my travels, as well as some family dishes that hold a special place in my life. Some were inspired by friends and others were inspired by ingredients, and some of them are recipes from my show. These days it seems everyone has more and more demands on their time So I took into consideration the person with an active lifestyle and made these recipes simple, with ingredients that can be found in any well-stocked supermarket.

I hope you enjoy making these recipes as much as I've enjoyed creating them. Feel free to change things up and experiment, or make the recipes exactly as they are. Just remember one of the most important ingredients is people. With less and less time, it becomes so important to create and keep creating memorable moments with friends and family. So make some time to cook something with them or just for yourself.

Ok, no more talking . . . step into my kitchen and grab a cocktail because it's time to get our cook on!!

SETTING UP YOUR KITCHEN BRIAN'S WAY

Whoever said it's the poor craftsman who blames his tools never had to cook in a badly equipped kitchen. I really believe that to cook your best, and to enjoy it as much as you should, you need the right equipment, a properly stocked pantry, and a few simple strategies for success. You don't have to have a restaurant-quality setup, just the right essentials to make everything easier and quicker. It all starts with the gear.

KNIVES: Don't stint on knives. That's pretty much my philosophy for all kitchen equipment, but where knives are concerned, quality means better cutting, faster food prep, and—most important—better safety. Superior knives also stay sharp longer than cheaper versions. Although there are high-quality knife sets out there, you don't necessarily need a full set. I use three knives for about 90 percent of my food prep: a large chef's knife, a smaller version, and a serrated knife. When picking out a knife to use for general prep, find one with a bowed bottom edge (what we call a "rocker" in skating), which will make chopping a lot easier and less tiring.

MINI CHOPPER: I'm a big fan of a simple as-seen-on-TV food chopper. Chop garlic, onions, herbs, and more in a fraction of the time using a knife would take, and impress your friends and family in the process!

POTS AND PANS: The best cookware heats evenly and prevents food from sticking. Flimsy pots and pans will have hot spots that make it nearly impossible to maintain consistency in your dishes. I like copper-clad stainless steel pots and pans for general use, and a large or small frying pan (sometimes called an omelet pan) for when I want to create a crispy surface on food such as fish without the food sticking. I also have a cast-iron skillet that is one of my favorite kitchen tools—especially for cooking meat or poultry. Cast iron heats uniformly and holds heat to cook food evenly. And when a cast-iron pan is properly seasoned (seasoning cast iron is the process of sealing the metal's pores by coating the clean surface with pure vegetable oil and then burning it off under low heat to make it non-stick), it will be almost as nonstick as Teflon.

KITCHEN BOWLS: I use bowls for two different purposes in my kitchen—and those purposes require two different types of bowls. For mixing, I prefer nonreactive stainless steel in at least four different sizes. For organizing measured ingredients prior to preparing a dish, I use what are known as *mise en place* bowls. Get yourself a stock of these in various sizes—choose glass or ceramic or even metal if that appeals to you (but stay away from plastic because plastic can affect the flavor of

certain ingredients). They're really inexpensive, and they can make food prep and cooking so much easier. It's a great way to have everything ready to go when you're cooking for friends, so that you don't spend a ton of time measuring and organizing when you should be mingling and partying!

PEPPERMILL: Freshly ground black pepper is essential to great cooking. That's why no kitchen is complete without a durable peppermill.

FOOD PROCESSOR: I have several different sizes of food processors, but really, you only need one with an extra-small bowl insert.

A PROPER PANTRY

There's nothing worse than getting ready to whip up your favorite recipe only to find that you're missing key ingredients. Avoid that by keeping your pantry stocked with basics that you use again and again. You don't necessarily have to have a separate pantry to set up a "pantry"—well-organized cabinet space will easily hold everything you'll need.

SALT: It really is the spice of life and crucial to most of the recipes you'll make. I use kosher salt because it's flaky and light, which translates to less sodium per measured amount. I also have a selection of flavored salts; they aren't essential for the home cook, but it's a great way to add unexpected flavors to certain dishes.

CANNED TOMATOES: I keep several 28-ounce cans of diced and crushed tomatoes on hand at all times.

SPICES: Avoid frustration by keeping a full set of spices in your pantry. Although most cooking involves a core group of four or five spices, it's always helpful to have others available when you need them, and you can experiment with them as well.

MUSTARDS: I always keep at least two types of mustard on hand—a quality Dijon and a grainy "country-style" mustard. However, there are tons of different styles, and using these can be a great low-fat, high-flavor way to perk up dishes from meats to salads.

STOCKS: I keep chicken and vegetable stock "stocked" and ready for soups, stews, and other dishes. I like the convenience of packaged liquid stocks, but you can use bouillon cubes if you prefer (and they take up less space).

PARMESAN!: To my mind, you aren't really cooking if you don't have a hunk of Parmesan cheese somewhere in your kitchen.

THE BOITANO SAUCE, SALSA, AND SPREAD PLAN

Saving time in the kitchen is really important to me because of my busy life-style. I'm always looking for ways to be more efficient. One of the strategies I developed a long time ago is to make larger portions of sauces, spreads, and salsas than are necessary for whatever recipe I'm making. I store the extra amounts and use them to accent meat, fish, and even sandwiches. I'll use one or two of the spreads or sauces for a week or two, and then rotate in a new one. You can even take a free afternoon, if you have one, and make several of the accompaniments below and stockpile them.

Red Pepper Relish, page 8 | Red Onion Jam, page 48 | Plum Salsa, page 126
Red Chimichurri Sauce, page 130 | Pea-and-Basil Pesto, page 158
Green Salsa page 112

STARTERS

I LIKE TO CALL THESE DISHES "STARTERS" because I don't use them just as appetizers and there are lots of ways you can go with them. Try making a simple, tasty nosh before you and your date head out the door, or gather a few friends and hang out in the kitchen with some cocktails for an informal meal of starters. Or use a starter in the traditional way—as the first course for a sit-down dinner.

Some starters are better suited for stand-alone service, while others fit more elegantly into a multicourse meal. The recipes here are grouped into two different categories: "Tempting Tapas" and "Simple and Sophisticated." I interpret tapas as being more casual. They are often eaten as snacks and with your fingers (like the White Bean, Caramelized Onion, and Artichoke Bruschetta on page 6). The more simple and sophisticated appetizers work best as the first course for a sit-down meal, like the Smoked Salmon with Lemon Crème Fraîche and Capers on page 18.

TEMPTING TAPAS

Tapas—both the word and the idea—originated in Spain but have pretty much spread across the globe. You don't need to know Spanish to speak the language of tapas. Tapa is Spanish for "cover" or "lid," and legend has it that the first tapas were flat pieces of crusty bread placed across the top of bar drinks to keep flies out of sweet Spanish sherry. Nowadays, the term describes quick and simple bar snacks that can be eaten with a drink or two, or combined with other tapas to make a casual and tasty meal.

My love affair with tapas began on my first to visit to Spain. I spent six weeks in Seville, working on the film *Carmen on Ice*. The filming took place all over the city. The crew would lay down ice over a different square where we would then film a different scene for the movie. We even skated in the vast Plaza de Toros de la Real Maestranza, Seville's famous bullring, and a tiny Tabac factory like the cigarette factory where Carmen worked in the story.

A couple weeks before Christmas, it began raining and just didn't stop. Ten straight days of rain! It was the rainiest period the city had seen in fifty years. We were shooting outside, so they had to suspend production. That gave me the chance to do some last-minute Christmas shopping and take a taste-bud tour of Seville. Every afternoon I'd trek out to see a different area of the city, but I kept returning to a couple of the city's nicest squares, like Plaza del Duque in the city's center. The shopping was great, but it was really all the incredible restaurants around the edges of the square that kept luring me back.

I made a habit of having a predinner drink with a couple of friends from the cast every night, along with a few tapas—chunks of potato with spicy mayonnaise, meat skewers, or simple chorizo served with delicious country bread. My favorite tapas were the *boquerones*—fried sardines. Besides the incredible flavor and crunch, the great thing about *boquerones* is that they are an acquired taste; I thought I wouldn't have to worry too much about sharing. As it turns out, everyone I was with discovered they loved the flavor just as much as I did.

All those tapas taught me a lot about the magic of simple, earthy flavors—a magic I've tried to re-create in dishes like the Polenta with Spicy Sausage and Red Pepper Relish on page 8. Create your own magic and capture the fun and casual atmosphere of a Spanish bar by gathering a few close friends, pouring some cocktails, and whipping up a few of the recipes like the Southwestern Sopapillas on page 10.

PAELLA SLIDERS

Some of the best appetizers and tapas are made by downsizing more substantial dishes, and that was the idea behind this recipe. Miniaturizing makes this recipe an ideal tapa because you can pop it in your mouth in one or two bites, and it's way less messy to eat than the full-size version. I wanted to pay homage to my friend Yvonne's mom, Manuela. She is like an adopted grandmother, and she makes an awesome paella. I deconstructed her paella and incorporated some of the fabulous ingredients from her traditional paella—spicy chorizo, richly flavored scallops, and lots of garlic—and re-created it in the form of a burger. She loved it!

SERVES 4–6 (20 SMALL BURGERS)

SPICY PIMENTO MAYO:

1 cup mayonnaise

1 teaspoon chili powder

1 tablespoon lemon juice

1 (4-ounce) jar pimentos, chopped
    fine, juice reserved

BURGERS:

1 pound ground chicken

½ pound Mexican-style chorizo
    sausage, removed from casing

½ pound sea scallops, chopped

1 tablespoon tomato paste

3 cloves garlic, chopped fine

2 tablespoons chopped fresh parsley
    leaves

1 teaspoon salt

½ teaspoon freshly ground black
    pepper

20 mini rolls

10 butter lettuce leaves, torn in half

4 plum tomatoes, sliced thin

1. Combine all the ingredients for the spicy pimento mayo, including the reserved pimento juice, in a small bowl. Set aside.

2. Combine all the burger ingredients, except the rolls, lettuce, and tomatoes, in a large bowl and mix well. (Smush them with your hands!)

3. Form the mixture into small patties about 2 inches in diameter, and arrange on a platter lined with waxed paper. Cover with plastic wrap and refrigerate until ready to grill.

BRIAN'S KITCHEN POINTER

Here's the skinny on chorizo. There are many types, but two basic styles: Mexican and Spanish. Spanish chorizo is the original, made with dried red peppers and paprika, and cured, smoked, or left *uncooked* as *chorizo fresco.* Cured and smoked versions are usually eaten as sliced meats. Mexican chorizo is made with dried and crushed chile peppers so it is hotter, and all Mexican chorizo is left uncooked in the style of chorizo fresco. Dishes like my Paella Sliders incorporate uncooked chorizo that is removed from the casing before use. Spanish chorizo tends to have a denser, smokier flavor, while Mexican-style is spicier and bit fattier. The Mexican version is often used as one of the "power ingredients" in a recipe, and needs strong flavors to hold up to it. Spanish chorizo is more of an ensemble ingredient that plays well in a diverse mix of flavors, such as in stews or paella.

4. Preheat the grill to medium-high. Oil the grill grates and put the burgers on the grill to cook for 4 minutes per side.

5. Transfer to a serving platter and serve on mini rolls with lettuce, tomato, and spicy pimento mayo.

BRIAN'S KITCHEN POINTER

If you want to make the surface a little more charred and crispy, chop the scallops into chunky sizes so that more of the scallop is exposed to the heat.

WHITE BEAN, CARAMELIZED ONION, *and* ARTICHOKE BRUSCHETTA

Classic bruschetta is an Italian favorite dating back centuries. Bread is toasted with olive oil and covered with one of many different types of toppings. I put a Middle Eastern spin on this version by using a base of healthy whole-wheat pita that toasts up to a satisfying crunch. It also makes for a pleasing combination of creamy and chunky textures. Half is done in the food processor and half in rough chop form. Not only is this appetizer delicious, it's also packed with protein, vitamins, and fiber.

SERVES 4-6 (32 PIECES)

2 whole-wheat pitas

7 tablespoons olive oil, divided

1 large yellow onion, sliced thin

Salt

1 (15-ounce) can artichoke hearts, packed in water and drained

1 (15.5-ounce) can cannellini beans, drained and rinsed

Juice of 1 lemon, divided

Freshly ground black pepper to taste

1 clove garlic, chopped

¼ teaspoon red pepper flakes

2 tablespoons chopped fresh parsley

1. Preheat the oven to 350°F.

2. Slice each pita in half to make 4 half-moons. Brush each with olive oil. Slice each half-moon into 6 wedges. Spread the wedges on a baking sheet. Toast in the oven for about 8 minutes. Let cool completely.

3. Heat 2 tablespoons of olive oil in a large skillet over medium-low heat. Add the sliced onion, season with salt, and cook until golden brown, about 20 minutes. Stir every few minutes.

4. While the onions are cooking, add half of the artichoke hearts and two-thirds of the beans to a food processor. Add 2 tablespoons of olive oil and half the lemon juice, and season with salt and pepper. Puree until smooth and set aside. Chop the remaining artichoke hearts.

5. When the onions are done cooking, turn the heat to medium and add 1 tablespoon of olive oil to the pan along with the garlic and red pepper flakes. Cook for 1 minute.

6. Add the remaining beans, artichoke hearts, and lemon juice. Season with salt and pepper and stir. Cook until heated through, remove from the heat, and let cool to room temperature.

7. Spread a heaping teaspoon of the bean-and-artichoke puree onto each pita wedge. Top each wedge with a dollop of the onion, bean, and artichoke mixture. Sprinkle with the chopped parsley and arrange on a platter to serve.

PLATE-LICKING GOOD

The first time I served White Bean, Caramelized Onion, and Artichoke Bruschetta was when I cooked a charity auction dinner at skating legend Dick Button's house in New York. He kept coming into the kitchen to make sure I was really making the meal. He must have liked it, because I snapped a photo of him licking his plate! He offered me a great tip that was handed down from his mother regarding dinner parties: Never throw away the trash until you have all the silverware put away. Invariably some of it ends up in the trash. Sure enough, we found a fork in the trashcan.

POLENTA *with* SPICY SAUSAGE *and* RED PEPPER RELISH

These little appetizers were a big hit at my friend Tony's party (see Sun-Dried Tomato and Goat Cheese Skewers on page 16). The crispy, pan-fried polenta is essential, but the key is the relish. It pulls the whole thing together. After we filmed that episode featuring the party, I found crew members eating the extra relish by the spoonful. Make a little extra relish to save for later—it's a great addition to sandwiches, hot dogs, and burgers. It will last up to a month in a sealed container in the refrigerator.

You can also grill the polenta squares. Brush them with olive oil and grill over medium heat for about 2 to 3 minutes per side.

SERVES 6

POLENTA:

2 tablespoons olive oil, divided

3 cups chicken broth

1 teaspoon salt

¼ teaspoon freshly ground black pepper

1 cup quick-cooking polenta

3 tablespoons grated Parmesan

1 pound spicy Italian sausage

2 cups canola oil

Fresh parsley leaves, for garnish

RED PEPPER RELISH:

2 small red peppers, diced fine

1 medium yellow onion, diced fine

¾ cup white vinegar

2 teaspoons mustard seeds

¼ cup sugar, plus 2 tablespoons

½ teaspoon salt

1. Brush a 9 × 13-inch baking sheet with 1 tablespoon olive oil and set aside.

2. Bring the chicken broth to a boil in a medium pot over medium heat. Add the salt, pepper, and polenta and whisk until thick, about 4 minutes.

3. Stir in the Parmesan and pour out onto the prepared baking sheet, spreading into a smooth layer. Cover with plastic wrap and refrigerate to set up, about 1 hour. (This can also be done the night before.)

4. Combine all the relish ingredients in a medium pot, with ¼ cup water. Cover and cook over medium heat for 30 minutes. Remove the cover and cook for another 30 minutes, or until thick. Cool to room temperature and transfer to a bowl. This will keep, up to 2 weeks, refrigerated in a sealed container.

5. Preheat the oven to 225°F.

6. Add the remaining tablespoon of olive oil to a large skillet over medium heat. Add the sausage and cook until brown on all sides, about 10 minutes. Transfer to a baking dish and put in the preheated oven to keep warm.

7. While the sausage is cooking, add the canola oil to a large skillet and heat over medium-high heat, around 350°F.

8. Remove the polenta from the refrigerator and cut into 1½-inch squares. Fry the polenta squares in batches until lightly browned and crispy, about 3 to 4 minutes per side. Transfer to a plate lined with paper towels.

9. Arrange the polenta on a serving platter. Slice the sausage into ½-inch-thick pieces and put on top of the fried polenta squares. Top with a dollop of red pepper relish and garnish with a fresh parsley leaf.

SOUTHWESTERN SOPAPILLAS

Sopapillas always sounds like "super pillows" to me, which is sort of what they are—flaky, delicate pillows of delicious fried dough. A traditional Mexican dessert, sopapillas are often paired with sweet accents, such as drizzled honey or fruit puree. But I wanted to try a savory filling because I liked the texture of the dough so much, and it makes the perfect backdrop for the fresh, piquant bite of this black bean salsa. The colors in this dish make for an eye-catching presentation, and the dough "pillow" is a perfect container for bite-size finger food.

SERVES 6–8 (36 PIECES)

BLACK BEAN SALSA:

1 (15-ounce) can black beans, drained and rinsed

2 Roma tomatoes, seeded and diced

1 (4-ounce) can roasted green chiles (recommended: Hatch)

1 clove garlic, chopped

1 avocado, peeled, halved, pitted, and diced

Juice of 1 lime

1½ teaspoons ancho chili powder

3 ounces (about ½ cup) crumbled *queso fresco*

2 tablespoons canola oil

Pinch of salt

Pinch of freshly ground black pepper

3 tablespoons chopped fresh cilantro

DOUGH:

3 cups all-purpose flour, plus extra for work surface

1 tablespoon baking powder

2 teaspoons salt, divided

¼ cup shortening

4 cups canola oil

1 teaspoon ancho chili powder

½ teaspoon freshly ground black pepper

1. Combine all the salsa ingredients into a bowl and toss to mix well. Set aside.

2. Sift together the flour, baking powder, and 1 teaspoon salt into a large bowl. Cut in the shortening with a fork or pastry blender. Add 1 to 1¼ cups room-temperature water gradually, until the dough comes together and forms a ball.

3. Turn the dough onto a floured surface and knead until smooth. Cover and let rest for 5 minutes. (The dough can also be made in a standing mixer.)

4. Heat the canola oil in a large high-sided skillet to 350°F.

5. Mix the remaining 1 teaspoon of salt, ancho chili powder, and pepper in a small bowl. Set aside.

6. Divide the dough into 4 equal portions. Roll each portion into a square about ¼-inch thick. Cut each piece into 2 × 2-inch squares.

7. Working in batches, carefully add about 6 pieces of the dough to the hot oil. Using tongs, turn the dough

BRIAN'S KITCHEN POINTER

If you can't find ancho chili powder, use regular chili powder instead. To give the salsa a spicy, smoky kick, add one chopped chipotle pepper. The salsa can be made a few hours ahead of time. Just make sure to cover the surface with plastic wrap and store it in the refrigerator.

frequently to ensure even puffing and cooking. Fry until golden brown. (They should puff up like little pillows.)

8. Remove sopapillas from the oil and drain on a sheet pan lined with paper towels. Sprinkle with a bit of the ancho chili mixture. Repeat with the remaining pieces of dough.

9. Transfer the fried dough to a serving tray. Puncture the tops slightly with a spoon. Top each with about a tablespoon of the salsa and serve.

BEEF SATAY

Satay is an Indonesian staple that got its start as a delectable fast food offered by Javanese street vendors for workers in a hurry. For what appears to be such a simple dish, the flavors are complex—a perfect combination of tart and sweet. The marinated meat grills up juicy and tender. Some satays are served with sauces, but this one is so richly seasoned that a sauce isn't necessary, and it's just that much easier to prepare without one.

SERVES 4 (16 PIECES)

1 pound flatiron steak

½ cup soy sauce

¼ cup vegetable broth

Juice of 1 lime

2 teaspoons hot sauce (recommended: Sriracha)

1 tablespoon rice wine vinegar

2 tablespoons vegetable oil

1 tablespoon honey

2 cloves garlic, chopped

1 teaspoon chopped fresh ginger

3 scallions, sliced and divided

3 tablespoons chopped fresh cilantro, divided

16 (8-inch) bamboo skewers, soaked in water for 30 minutes

1. Slice beef against the grain into ½-inch-thick strips. Place into a large, heavy-duty, resealable bag.

2. Whisk together all the remaining ingredients, except 1 sliced scallion and 1 tablespoon chopped cilantro, in a small bowl. Pour into the resealable bag with the beef, seal the bag, and toss to coat completely. Place the bag into a large bowl and refrigerate for at least 1 hour, or as long as overnight.

3. Preheat the grill or a grill pan over medium-high heat.

4. Thread the beef strips onto skewers.

5. Oil the grill grates or grill pan and cook skewers 2 to 3 minutes per side.

6. Remove from the grill and place on a serving platter. Sprinkle with the reserved sliced scallion and chopped cilantro. Serve immediately.

BRIAN'S KITCHEN POINTER

Flank or skirt steak also works well in this recipe. The satay can also be cooked under a broiler. Place a sheet pan lined with foil under the broiler to preheat. Once the tray is hot, place the skewers on it and broil for 2 to 3 minutes per side.

SIMPLE & SOPHISTICATED

Paris. It's a word full of magic. It is a foodie's dream. Everywhere you go, there's something to make you hungry. Walk down any street, and you might run right smack into the aroma of freshly baked baguettes, or be treated to the sight of a thousand cheeses in a fromagerie's window display.

The first time I visited Paris, I stayed at the Hôtel de Crillon, right off the Champs Élysées. It was by far the ritziest place I had ever stayed, up to that point in my life. It was a classic French hotel, and you couldn't lift a finger without someone appearing out of thin air to do whatever it was you needed done. They had real down comforters on the beds (it may not sound impressive now, but at the time no hotel in the States had them). Oh, and they had this incredible hot chocolate, like no other hot chocolate I had ever tasted.

FRENCH DELIGHT

Here's how to make hot chocolate, French-style. Be warned, though: Taste this once, and you'll never be able to drink that packaged stuff again.

CHOCOLAT CHAUD
SERVES 2

2 cups whole milk

3 tablespoons water

3 tablespoons granulated sugar

1/3 teaspoon chili powder

Pinch of sea salt

6 ounces bittersweet chocolate
(I use Ghirardelli 70% Cacao Extra Bittersweet Chocolate Baking Bar)

1/3 teaspoon real vanilla extract

Combine the milk, water, sugar, chili powder, and salt in a medium saucepan over medium heat, stirring until the sugar is melted. Let the mixture come to a boil, remove from the heat, and whisk in the chocolate. Add the vanilla at the end. Serve immediately, adding more sugar as desired.

CRAB-*and*-AVOCADO CROSTINI

One of the first times I served this dish was for a *Los Angeles Times* food interview. This was one of my first interviews regarding food, and I was nervous because I was in someone else's kitchen and it was really, really small. It turned out to be the right recipe to serve, however, because to prepare it, I only needed the ingredients, a knife, a spoon, and a bowl. You can't get simpler than that.

This easy-to-make appetizer is proof that you can eat and entertain well while still leading an active lifestyle. It may look to your friends like you spent a long time preparing this dish, but you can throw it together in no time at all and it's really impressive when served. The tastes are phenomenal—smooth, creamy, and soft consistencies coupled with hard and crunchy textures, and the tangy zest mixes with pleasant, mild sweetness.

SERVES 6

1 loaf *ficelle,* or thin French baguette

3 tablespoons olive oil, plus ¼ cup

Juice of 1 Meyer lemon or mix equal parts lemon juice and orange juice as a substitute

Salt and freshly ground black pepper to taste

1 yellow pepper, seeded and diced

1 avocado, peeled, halved, pitted, and diced

1 shallot, diced fine

8 ounces fresh lump crabmeat

1. Preheat the oven to 400°F.

2. Slice the bread into ½-inch-thick slices. Lightly brush the slices with 3 tablespoons of olive oil. Arrange the bread on a baking sheet fitted with a rack and bake until lightly toasted, about 8 minutes. Remove from the oven and let cool before topping with the crab mixture.

3. Whisk together the lemon juice, ¼ cup of olive oil, and salt and pepper in a large bowl. Add the yellow pepper, avocado, shallot, and crabmeat and toss gently, being careful not to break up the crabmeat.

4. Top the bread slices with about a tablespoon of the crab mixture and arrange on a serving platter.

BRIAN'S KITCHEN POINTER

Canned crabmeat won't cut it for this recipe, or any recipe for that matter—it really doesn't taste as good as its fresh counterpart. Always buy fresh lump crabmeat, available at the seafood counter at upscale grocery stores or from a seafood shop. And absolutely no k-r-a-b, that super-high-sodium, pressed whitefish real-crab substitute.

SUN-DRIED TOMATO *and* GOAT CHEESE SKEWERS

On one episode of *What Would Brian Boitano Make?* I made this simple, lip-smacking finger food as an hors d'oeuvre for a party I threw for my friend Tony, when I was trying to find him the perfect girlfriend. The party was all about pairing, and so was the food. The creamy, smooth goat cheese pairs well with the satisfying crunch of the pistachios. It's also super easy to make—a lot easier than it was for Tony to find that one special woman out of the seventeen I invited. He did find his partner . . . she just wasn't one of the women at the party (you can't blame the food, though!).

SERVES 4-6 (20 SKEWERS)

1 (8-ounce) log fresh goat cheese, chilled

1 cup finely chopped pistachio nuts

20 sun-dried tomatoes packed in oil

½ bunch fresh basil leaves

20 small skewers or long cocktail toothpicks

1. Fill a pitcher with hot water. Dip a knife into the hot water and slice the goat cheese log in half lengthwise. Slice each half into 10 pieces, making sure to dip the knife into the hot water in between slicing to ensure a nice, clean cut.

2. Roll each piece of goat cheese into a ball approximately ½ inch in diameter and place on a cookie sheet lined with waxed paper.

3. Place the chopped pistachio nuts into a shallow bowl. Roll a goat cheese ball into the pistachio nuts, coating half the ball. Return the ball to the sheet pan and repeat with the remaining goat cheese balls.

4. Drain the oil from the tomatoes and set on a plate lined with a paper towel.

5. Slide a goat cheese ball onto a skewer. Lay a basil leaf on top of a sun-dried tomato. Fold the tomato in half around the basil leaf and slide it onto the skewer above the goat cheese. Repeat with the remaining skewers.

6. Arrange on a serving platter with half the balls face up and the other face down, cover, and keep refrigerated until ready to serve.

SMOKED SALMON *with* LEMON CRÈME FRAÎCHE *and* CAPERS

While I was in Paris, I learned a lot about how the French prepare and present an appetizer and how important that can be. This elegant starter would be right at home in a white-tablecloth restaurant, and it is the perfect first course for a high-style, sit-down dinner party. This presentation is great for entertaining because it looks like a rosebud made of salmon, perched on top of a dollop of lemony cream and resting on a fresh slice of cucumber. When you serve this, your guests will feel like they are eating something really special.

SERVES 4

4 ounces cream cheese, softened

½ cup crème fraîche, divided

1 tablespoon mayonnaise

1 tablespoon chopped capers

1 tablespoon finely diced shallot

1 teaspoon fresh lemon juice

1 tablespoon chopped fresh dill, plus more for garnish

Salt to taste

Pinch of white pepper

1 teaspoon lemon zest

1 (8-ounce) package smoked salmon

1 English cucumber

1. Mix the cream cheese, one-quarter (2 tablespoons) of the crème fraîche, the mayonnaise, capers, shallot, lemon juice, and dill in a medium bowl. Season with salt and white pepper. Taste and add more salt if necessary. Cover and refrigerate until ready to use.

2. Combine the remaining crème fraîche and lemon zest in a small bowl. Cover and refrigerate until ready to use.

3. Slice the salmon into strips about 1 inch wide and 2½ inches long. Roll up each strip to form a small rosette. Place on a plate, cover, and refrigerate until ready to use.

4. Slice the cucumber into ½-inch-thick slices. Use a melon baller or spoon to scoop out a small amount of the center of each slice, forming a small cup. Be careful not to go all the way through the slice.

5. Spoon 2 teaspoons of the cream cheese mixture into each cucumber cup. Place a salmon rosette on each filled cucumber cup.

6. Top each rosette with a small dollop of the crème fraîche mixture and serve.

BEVERAGES

ACCORDING TO MY FRIEND LISA, "There are drinks, and there are cocktails." I love making and enjoying both! Lisa says that drinks are all about simplicity, refreshment, and being casual—the pure taste of a single spirit or a simple combination of a spirit and a mixer casually stirred together. They are just the thing for informal family gatherings—the perfect way to enjoy down time and really relax.

Cocktails, on the other hand, Lisa says, are a celebration of being an adult, and they usually involve a shaker. And sometimes pretending like you are sophisticated. They can be like small science projects where you have to figure out the perfect balance of the spirit: sweet, bitter, tart, and sometimes effervescence. There is just no end to all the combinations you can use. It's sort of like cocktail pi.

I'm definitely the one who instigates happy hour in my family, even though my sister Jill can put away the pink wine and my sister Lynn never says no to a rum cocktail. And then there are my parents. I always remember watching my mom and dad get ready to go out dancing, and how sensational they looked dressed to the nines. They'd usually have a highball first—Old Crow bourbon with a splash of water, served in a tall glass (that's where the name "highball" comes from). At ten years old, I couldn't stand the smell of bourbon (age has its benefits—I've come to really appreciate bourbon's charms), but I loved the clink of ice in a glass as Dad made those drinks. That sound still embodies the promise of fun to me.

Whether you're making hot-weather drinks like the refreshing Watermelon Margarita on page 26 or you're going more highbrow with a cocktail like the smoky, sophisticated Calhoun on page 32, you'll need a few pieces of special equipment; see page 33 for more on the basics of bar gear.

BRIAN'S KITCHEN POINTER

Don't be confused by the "ounce" measurements I use in these recipes. One liquid ounce equals 2 tablespoons. More commonly, drink amounts are measured with a "jigger," a metal bar tool shaped like an hourglass. The cup on one side holds 1½ ounces when full (the amount of a precise "shot"). The other side holds 1 ounce. If you don't happen to have a real jigger, you can fill a shot glass ¾ full to measure an ounce. You can also substitute the word part for ounce—which gives you the flexibility to control the power of the alcohol or any other ingredient in the drink.

PURE REFRESHMENT

Summers in my family mean gathering every chance we get at my Aunt Tree's beach house, perched on the cliffs just outside Santa Cruz, California. The house has been handed down to the next generation and remains a great family meeting place, keeping Aunt Tree's memory alive. The house itself is just a simple old bungalow really, but it's incredibly comfortable and it sits on a tall bluff looking out over the Pacific Ocean. You can't beat the view or the memories we've accumulated there.

You wouldn't believe how many Boitanos we can cram into that little place. But no matter how many people there are, we all look to unwind and relax whenever we're together. That usually means doing nothing but enjoying each other's company, eating lots of delicious food, and partaking in a drink or four.

That's just the way my Aunt Tree liked it. She and Uncle George actually had a tiny bar set up in the corner of the patio. The bar had a bell over it. If you wanted a drink, you would just ring the bell and Uncle George would come and make it for you. There was a clock next to the bell with the number 6 in place of all the numbers on the face. Underneath there was a sign that said COCKTAIL HOUR STARTS AT SIX! Aunt Tree and Uncle George were old school in the best possible way.

My aunt and uncle are a big reason why I love to riff on classic drinks like margaritas, daiquiris, and lemon drops. Their cocktail hours inspired me to play with fascinating flavor blends, such as the unusually colorful citrus element in the Blood Orange Mojito on page 30. You can do your own experimenting by using the liquor as the base and layering flavors on top like you would paint on a canvas. Make your own creative quaff that refreshes and impresses your guests, and my Aunt Tree, being the consummate hostess that she was, will be grinning ear to ear.

WATERMELON MARGARITA

Margaritas are the classic summer cocktail, and I love classics. I especially enjoy the challenge of switching them up a little. I came up with this drink when my friend Kristi Yamaguchi brought her entire family over to my house for dinner. They have a lot of kids in the family, so I liked the fact that I could do a virgin version for them. The watermelon provides a clean, light sweetness that mellows the bite of the tequila. It also adds a freshness that counteracts the sometimes syrupy nature of this particular drink.

Margaritas are traditionally served in a wide shallow glass with a salted rim. Take that idea a step further and coat the rim with chili-spiked salt held in place with a coating of triple sec. The extremes of spicy, salty, and super sweet in this drink are a great refreshing combination.

SERVES 4

4 cups cubed watermelon

2 tablespoons granulated sugar

3 limes, 2 juiced and 1 cut into wedges for garnish

8 ounces tequila

5 ounces triple sec, divided

3 tablespoons salt

1 teaspoon chili powder

1. Puree the watermelon and sugar in a blender until smooth. Strain the puree through a fine-mesh sieve or cheesecloth.

2. Transfer the puree liquid to a pitcher and add the lime juice, tequila, and 4 ounces of the triple sec. Stir to combine.

3. Thoroughly mix the salt with the chili powder in a shallow dish. Put the remaining ounce of triple sec in a separate, smaller saucer.

4. Dip the rim of each margarita glass in the triple sec, then press it into the salt-and-chili mixture, twisting the glass slightly.

5. Divide the margarita between the 4 glasses, and garnish each with a lime wedge.

WHITE WINE SANGRIA

A couple of years after going to Spain to film the movie *Carmen on Ice,* I wound up returning with my family. We rented a house on the Costa del Sol, in a small village called Estepona. It was so picturesque that it was easy to understand why the region is called the "Spanish Riviera." Most nights we'd take a short drive north to Puerto Banus, a wealthy seaport just outside the town of Marbella. We would find a restaurant in the port with tables looking out over rows of incredible yachts, or a bar with a view of Gibraltar. But no matter where we went, we were in the right place for a pitcher or two of sangria and some delicious tapas.

One day at lunch we ordered a pitcher of white wine sangria, which was a little unusual—most sangrias are red. It was refreshing and sweet, just what we were all in the mood for. This is my version of that memorable sangria. The pitcher is filled with fruit, so it looks festive, beautiful, and super refreshing. The impact of the sweet fruit and white wine balance the bite of the citrus and the fizz of the seltzer water. This sangria has a nice, clean finish that makes it a great match for grilled fish or chicken, or a meal of light tapas.

SERVES 8

1 (750-ml) bottle dry Spanish white wine (any light, dry white wine will work, but I like a nice Verdejo or Albarino)

¼ cup superfine sugar

1 lime, sliced thin

1 lemon, sliced thin

1 Granny Smith apple, cored and sliced thin

1½ cups seedless green grapes, sliced in half

1 cup apple juice

½ bunch fresh mint leaves

Pinch of salt

1 (12-ounce) can seltzer water

1. In a large pitcher, combine the wine and sugar, stirring until the sugar dissolves completely.

2. Add the remaining ingredients, except the seltzer, and mix well. Put the pitcher in the refrigerator and let the sangria sit for at least 1 hour, and up to 4 hours.

3. Just before serving, add ice cubes to just below the top of the pitcher, pour in the seltzer, and stir well.

BLOOD ORANGE MOJITO

I love the sweet taste and beautiful color of blood oranges, and I have always wanted to use one in a drink. When I decided to throw a Cuban Salsa party for my friend Renee, I knew it was my opportunity. This drink features an appealing mix of sweet and tart. Blood orange also brings a slight undertone of berry to the orange citrus flavor, which makes the taste a little more complex. Part of the magic of a drink is the way it looks, and this drink looks as good as it tastes, with its vibrant orange-red hue and accent of green mint. Although the traditional mojito is made with sparkling water, try club soda for just a bit of saltiness to cut the rum's sweetness. Here's my twist on a Cuban mojito using a blood orange.

SERVES 4

1 blood orange, cut into wedges

1 lime, cut into wedges

12 mint leaves, plus 4 sprigs for garnish

¼ cup granulated sugar

4 shots white rum

1 (12-ounce) can club soda

1. Divide the fruit wedges, mint leaves, and sugar evenly among 4 large highball glasses.

2. Muddle the fruit with a wood muddler, or the back of a large spoon, until the juice has been extracted.

3. Add a shot of rum to each glass and stir.

4. Fill each glass with ice. Top with club soda, stir thoroughly, and serve garnished with a mint sprig.

SUPERCHIC COCKTAILS

For me, the idea of cocktails always brings to mind great old-school restaurants. The East Coast hallmark golden-era restaurant is the Rainbow Room, a place full of sepia-toned charm. Big bands played the Rainbow Room, and every table had a perfect view of the stunning New York skyline. A night at the Rainbow Room meant incredible food, powerful cocktails, and endless dancing.

San Francisco's version is the Top of the Mark, the restaurant that occupies the penthouse of the InterContinental Mark Hopkins hotel. The Top of the Mark was originally designed in 1939

as a "cocktail lounge," and may actually be the definitive place for cocktails and dancing. Many nights you can find a different jazz or swing band on the bill, and the panoramic view makes you feel like you're actually on top of the city. Both my mom and dad are incredible dancers, and they used to go there on dates.

The last time my family went to the Top of the Mark was for my mom's eightieth birthday. It was a magical night, summed up in a snapshot moment right before we took the elevator down to leave. My mother, looking incredibly elegant in her most beautiful dress, grabbed my father's hand and they began to jitterbug right in front of the elevators. I captured that dance on video, and it symbolizes everything my parents are about—their sense of style, their simple joy of life that go hand in hand with their love of San Francisco.

A cocktail can capture that type of magic and be an amazing taste sensation when you hit on just the right combination of sour, sweet, smoky, and smooth, like the Marky DV on page 33. The right cocktail takes me back to the best of San Francisco, and how it made my parents want to dance and fall more in love every night.

THE CALHOUN

I invented this drink for my friend Jack, who has an incredible, custom-made bar in his house filled with lots and lots of bottles chosen strictly for their design. Jack has a lot of parties. One night at one of his parties, I decided to create a drink we could serve at more of his soirees. I used what was on hand and came up with an interesting mix of flavors. Lots of cordials are just overwhelmingly sweet and syrupy, but the St. Germaine liqueur in this cocktail is made from elderflower blossoms used within hours of picking, which translates to a bright floral flavor. I added two kinds of citrus to keep it fresh and lively. The Cointreau adds just enough sweetness and flavor to make it go down smoothly.

SERVES 1

2 ounces vodka

1 ounce St. Germaine (elderflower liqueur)

1 ounce Cointreau

Splash of fresh lemon juice

Splash of fresh lime juice

Lemon peel, for garnish

1. Combine the ingredients into a cocktail shaker filled three-quarters full of ice. Shake and pour into a chilled martini glass.

2. Garnish with a lemon peel dropped into the drink and serve.

BRIAN'S KITCHEN POINTER

Cocktail parties are about having fun, not working all night! So when you throw a party, multiply a recipe like The Calhoun for the number of people you'll be serving, and then mix all the ingredients in a pitcher before the party—no ice. When it comes time to serve the drinks, stir the mixture in the pitcher and use it to fill a shaker, pouring the drinks as needed. It's an easy and quick way to get back to the party and on with the fun!

MARKY DV

My friend Mark is a bartender, and he knows I love bourbon. One day I told him to surprise me, and this is what he came up with. I liked this drink so much that I asked him if I could "borrow" it for my cookbook—all of which explains the name. I like the strong, warm bite of the bourbon and brandy, mellowed just a little bit by the pear essence, with a hint of sweetness and faint whiff of orange. The bourbon dominates as bourbon will do, so this is a drink for people who like their bourbon.

SERVES 1

2½ ounces Maker's Mark bourbon

1½ ounces pear brandy

½ ounce simple syrup

4 dashes orange bitters

Combine the ingredients in a cocktail shaker filled three-quarters full of ice. Shake for 5 seconds and pour into a chilled martini glass.

BAR GEAR 101

Making great cocktails will be a lot easier if your bar is stocked with the appropriate tools. Many of these can do double-duty in the kitchen.

COCKTAIL SHAKER. This is a stainless steel canister with a removable lid that has a strainer built into it. It makes mixing and chilling cocktails a snap. And frankly, cocktail shakers just look cool.

STRAINER. Most cocktail shakers have a strainer built right into the lid, but a separate strainer can be handy for straining out fruit pulp or other ingredients. The stainless steel bar strainer has a small paddle head with a spring coil running around the edge that makes it easy to secure over the mouth of a shaker.

BAR SPOON. This is a special long utensil with a sturdy handle that won't bend, and a small spoon at one end. Some have a muddler on the opposite end.

MUDDLER. A muddler is the bar equivalent of a pestle, a thick miniature wood club with a rounded end. It's used to crush certain drink ingredients, such as fresh mint, in the bottom of a glass.

BOTTLE OPENER AND CHURCH KEY. A basic bottle opener is an essential bar tool for removing non-screw-off type bottle caps. A church key is a similar tool with a sharp, downward-curved point at one end. It's used to open cans of fluid ingredients. Do yourself a favor and buy a combination tool with a bottle opener at one end and a church key at the other.

WINE OPENER. Choose between a corkscrew style or an Ah-So wine opener. Corkscrews are more popular and easier to use; you just screw the point down into the cork, and wedge the cork up out of the bottle's neck. An Ah-So opener has two thin legs joined by a handle. The legs are wedged down on opposite sides of the cork, between the cork and the lip of the bottle. The cork is then twisted out.

LEMON MERINGUE

One of my favorite flavors in a cocktail is anything citrus. This drink is all about the lemon. Its centerpiece is the classic Italian cordial Limoncello. Limoncello is made from clear alcohol, lemon zest, and sugar, and it is often sipped on its own as an aperitif. In this drink, it ties together the pleasingly smooth sweet syrup, the lightly tart lemon juice, and the punch of the vodka. The egg white makes it slightly frothy and binds all the tart and sweet flavors together. The rim garnish of crushed candy adds a surprising and festive element to the cocktail.

SERVES 1

5–7 Lemon Drop candies

1 lemon wedge

2 ounces vodka

2 ounces Limoncello

1 ounce fresh lemon juice

Splash of simple syrup

4 teaspoons pasteurized egg white,
    or about ½ fresh egg white

Lemon peel, for garnish

1. Place the Lemon Drop candies in a resealable bag and crush them with a rolling pin until they are the consistency of coarse sugar. Pour the crushed candies into a shallow saucer.

2. Wipe the rim of a chilled martini glass with a lemon wedge. Press the rim into the crushed candies, lightly twisting to coat the rim all the way around.

3. Combine all the remaining ingredients except for the lemon peel in a cocktail shaker filled three-quarters full of ice. Shake for 5 to 10 seconds.

4. Pour into the martini glass. Garnish with a lemon peel dropped into the drink and serve.

BRIAN'S KITCHEN POINTER

Simple syrup is a standard bartending ingredient that's used to sweeten and thicken many different cocktails. To make the syrup, melt granulated sugar in heated (not boiling) water. The traditional recipe calls for two parts sugar to one part water, but you can use a one-to-one ratio that is a little less cloying. As soon as the sugar has melted, let the mixture cool, and store in a sanitized bottle. The basic simple syrup is fine, but try making all kinds of flavors. For instance, when I was serving mint juleps for a Kentucky Derby party, rather than muddle fresh mint in each drink, I steeped some leftover mint stems in the hot simple syrup. Then I used the syrup to make the mint juleps! You can try infusing just about any flavor, such as lavender, orange, or even chili! Always taste-test flavored simple syrup before you use it in any drinks though!

ITALIAN 88

This is my version of the classic French 75 cocktail. That drink was developed in 1915, so it was definitely time for an update. The Prosecco is the Italian equivalent of champagne—effervescent, dry, and refreshing. A lump of sugar offsets the tartness of the grapefruit juice, providing some balance to a drink with a mix of well-rounded, clean flavors. You can serve it at brunch or at cocktail hour, but be warned: After just a couple of these, you'll understand why the original version was named for 75-millimeter artillery.

SERVES 6

6 shots chilled vodka

6 shots chilled pink grapefruit juice

1 bottle chilled Prosecco

6 sugar cubes

1. Line up 6 chilled champagne flutes. Add 1 shot of vodka to each flute, then add 1 shot of grapefruit juice.

2. Top off each flute with Prosecco and drop in a sugar cube. Serve immediately.

BRIAN'S KITCHEN POINTER

Mixing cocktails means working with ice, but ice can be a cocktail's enemy. Melted ice is water, and water dilutes the flavors of the cocktail. That's why professional bartenders mix drinks quickly in a cocktail shaker, shaking the drink for no more than 5 to 10 seconds. Have the ingredients you're going to use in the drink ready to go before you start mixing it, and always add nonalcoholic ingredients to the shaker first. That way, if you accidently measure incorrectly or mess up, you won't be sacrificing expensive alcohol.

PASSION FRUIT *and* MANGO MAR-TONY

I had a lot of fun with this cocktail on my Food Network show. I decided to do my version of the TV show *The Bachelor* for my friend Tony, and created this drink and called it a Mar-Tony after him. I served it with a swizzle stick sporting a photo of his face. He was totally surprised when he walked onto the set thinking he was the lone guest, only to be greeted by seventeen single ladies I'd invited to meet him.

This drink combines the best of vacation-on-the-beach exotic fruit flavors with the straightforward, smooth taste of vodka and a bite of citrus. Drinks this complex are best used as cocktail party fare or as an after-dinner drink with dessert (or even for dessert). The Mar-Tony has a fairly thick, dense body and a beautiful sunset orange color, with many layers of great flavors that put the drink firmly in the "sophisticated" corner.

SERVES 4

1 large ripe mango
1 cup passion fruit nectar
Juice of 1 lime
4 shots vodka

1. Peel, pit, and cut the mango into chunks. Reserve some for garnish.

2. Puree the mango, passion fruit nectar, and lime juice in a blender until smooth. Strain through a mesh strainer and set aside.

3. Combine 1 part vodka and 1 part of the mango and passion fruit puree in a cocktail shaker full of ice. Shake and strain into a chilled martini glass.

4. Repeat with the remaining ingredients, and garnish each glass with a piece of mango skewered on a swizzle stick.

SOUP & SANDWICH EXPRESS

I'VE ALWAYS THOUGHT OF THE COMBO OF A SOUP AND SANDWICH AS A PERFECT MEAL. Given half a chance, each is just as comfortable stepping out into the spotlight and being there on its own. Sandwiches can be a great meal on the go or post-workout, with protein, carbs, and veggies all bundled up in one complete package. Often soups are stand-alone dinners, or one light course among many in a sit-down meal. In any case, soups and sandwiches are both ideal comfort foods. Maybe that's why some of my fondest memories include simple meals made of a hearty, fulfilling sandwich or a satisfying, comforting soup. So make yourself a soup-and-sandwich combination. It'll be easy to prepare, easy to enjoy, easy to devour.

SATISFYING SANDWICHES

As a young skater in training, my school days tended to be pretty long. Most weekdays I would start school at 8:30 in the morning and finish around 2:30 in the afternoon. Then I would go straight to the rink and practice till 8:00 at night. It was a passion for me even at that young age, so it didn't really seem like work. But there's no getting around the fact that those were pretty full days (even though my Aunt Jackie jokes that I've never had a real job). At night, I'd finally get home only to face the dreaded stack of homework.

No kid—especially one who has put in a long day—wants to tackle homework. I just really wanted to come home from a full day's work, unwind, and watch some TV with a huge bowl of ice cream with chocolate sauce in front of me. Unfortunately, my homework had to be done, but one of the things that made hitting the books bearable was when my mom would have my favorite meal ready for me when I got home from practice: a bowl of soup and a po'boy sandwich.

Po'boys started out as cheap, good food for the cash-strapped working class in New Orleans. The name actually comes from the term "poor boy" sifted through a New Orleans accent. The Big Easy version is an incredible meal of Italian cold cuts or breaded and fried shrimp or oysters captured between two slabs of a uniquely New Orleans style of French bread that is salty and chewy on the inside and crunchy on the outside.

My mom's po'boy was made from sourdough bread, with layers of Swiss cheese, pickles, and salami inside. She'd wrap it in aluminum foil and keep it hot for me, and when I'd walk into the house, the smell of the warm sourdough bread would surround me. The sandwich was just begging to be eaten . . . melted cheese would be smothering the salami, in a bed of soft, warm sourdough. A few bites of that sandwich and I'd be good to go, ready to tackle algebra (which I never really tackled) or history—which is where I learned what the New Orleans working class ate! The Hot Italian Sausage Panini with Pickled Peppers on page 44 is a tribute to mom's po'boy and its gooey cheesiness, incredible crunch, and almost decadent smell.

GRILLED STEAK SANDWICH *with* GOAT CHEESE, DIJON, *and* ROASTED PEPPERS

A steak sandwich is a substantial, classic meal-in-one. The secret to making it memorable is a cut of meat that is full of flavor. Flank steak is sliced thin across the grain and is the perfect sandwich meat, one that—like most sandwich steak—goes naturally with all kinds of cheese. The goat cheese in this sandwich is subtler than most steak-sandwich cheeses, with some tartness to complement the steak. Experiment with different breads to really change the character of the sandwich; a traditional sourdough or artisan bread could certainly up the "wow" factor.

SERVES 4

1 pound flank steak

1 loaf crusty whole-wheat or whole-grain bread

3 tablespoons olive oil

1 clove garlic, cut in half

Salt and freshly ground black pepper to taste

1 (4-ounce) log goat cheese, softened

4 teaspoons Dijon mustard

1 (12-ounce) jar roasted red peppers, each pepper cut into 4 equal pieces

2 cups arugula

1. Set the steak out for 30 minutes before cooking, to allow it to warm to room temperature. Preheat the oven to 400°F. Preheat the grill or grill pan over medium-high heat.

2. Cut the bread into 8 slices, each ½ inch thick. Brush both sides of each slice with olive oil and lay them on a sheet pan fitted with a rack. Lightly toast in the oven for about 6 minutes. Allow the bread to cool enough to handle, then rub each slice with garlic.

3. Thoroughly season the steak on both sides with salt and pepper.

4. Brush the grill grates or pan with vegetable oil to prevent the steak from sticking. Grill the steak 3 to 4 minutes per side over medium-high heat. Let the steak rest for 5 minutes before slicing. Slice against the grain into ¼-inch-thick slices.

5. Spread goat cheese on 4 of the bread slices. Spread mustard on the remaining 4 slices of bread.

6. Place the sliced steak onto the mustard-coated bread. Top with the peppers, then the arugula. Sprinkle with salt and pepper, and top with the goat cheese–coated bread slices. Slice the sandwiches diagonally and serve.

HOT ITALIAN SAUSAGE PANINI *with* PICKLED PEPPERS

This sandwich you can eat with your eyes, because it looks so good and it also packs a big punch. The sausage brings a hearty spiciness and satisfying pop to the panini, and the pickled peppers add a zing of tart flavor. The two cheeses have different melting points and very different flavors that complement the sausage. The provolone is subtler and melts to a nice creaminess, while the Parmesan has a firmer structure and more pronounced saltiness. It's my favorite snack for when my nieces and nephews come over and I need something quick, simple, and tasty to serve.

SERVES 6

PICKLED PEPPERS:

1½ cups white vinegar

½ teaspoon red pepper flakes

2 teaspoons salt

1 tablespoon granulated sugar

2 cloves garlic, smashed

1 red bell pepper, seeded and sliced

1 green bell pepper, seeded and sliced

1 medium yellow onion, sliced

SAUSAGE PANINI:

1 pound (about 6 links) hot Italian sausage, butterflied

6 ciabatta rolls, or 1 loaf of ciabatta bread cut into 6 portions

6 tablespoons olive oil

¼ pound, or 6 thin slices, provolone

¼ pound Parmesan, shaved

PICKLED PEPPERS:

1. Combine the white vinegar, 1½ cups water, red pepper flakes, salt, sugar, and garlic in a large pot and bring to a boil over medium heat.

2. When the mixture begins boiling, remove the pot from the heat and add the sliced peppers and onions. Let the ingredients pickle at room temperature for about 30 minutes. (The peppers will last up to 1 month in a resealable container stored in the refrigerator.)

SAUSAGE PANINI:

1. Preheat an outdoor grill or a grill pan over medium-high heat. Arrange the butterflied sausages on the grill, cut-side down. Cover the sausages with a sheet pan and weigh it down with a teakettle filled with water or a heavy skillet. Grill for 4 to 5 minutes per side.

2. Slice the rolls in half and brush them, inside and out, with the olive oil. Layer a slice of provolone over the bottom half of each roll. Add the cooked sausages on top of the cheese, then top with some of the pickled peppers and onions. Finish with 3 pieces of shaved Parmesan, and cover with the top half of each roll.

3. Place the sandwiches in a panini press, 2 or 3 at a time. Cook until the bread is crisp and the cheeses are melted, about 4 to 5 minutes. Transfer the sandwiches to a serving platter and serve.

BRIAN'S KITCHEN POINTER

No panini press? No problem! Grill these sandwiches in a large skillet over medium heat and put a cast-iron or heavy-bottomed pan on the sandwiches to flatten them. You can heat the cast iron skillet first to help accelerate the cooking process. Cook for 3 minutes per side. You won't have the distinctive grill marks on the bread, but the sandwiches will be every bit as delicious.

HAM, BRIE, *and* APPLE BUTTER PANINI

I used a classic Parisian cafe sandwich as inspiration for this breaded mouthsterpiece. The French take their sandwiches pretty seriously, because it's their version of fast food. This panini is quick to prepare and features subtle flavors and textures. The surprise is the use of the apple butter rather than the traditional sliced apples. I don't know about you, but I hate taking a bite of a sandwich with apples sliding out the side. This sandwich is both sweet and salty, with a slight peppery bite from the watercress. You can use any kind of mustard, but for my money, you can't top the spiciness and pop of grainy country mustard. This is a great centerpiece for a brunch with friends, especially when you pair it with my White Wine Sangria (page 28). And you'll also get your fruit quota for the day.

SERVES 2

½ French baguette

2 tablespoons olive oil

3 tablespoons apple butter

2 tablespoons whole-grain mustard (or Dijon, as preferred)

⅓ pound deli ham, sliced thin

1 cup watercress

¼ pound brie, sliced into 4 pieces

1. Slice the baguette in half lengthwise. Brush the outside of each half with olive oil. Spread the inside of one half of the bread with the apple butter and the other half with mustard.

2. Layer the ham on the bottom half of the baguette, then top with watercress and the brie. Top with the top half of the baguette and slice in half.

3. Cook the sandwiches in a panini press until the bread is crisp and cheese is melted, about 4 to 5 minutes. (If you do not have a panini press, see page 45 for an alternate method.)

4. Slice each panini in half diagonally, place on a plate, and serve.

GRILLED CHEESE SANDWICH *with* RED ONION JAM

I grew up eating the classic American version of the grilled cheese sandwich: margarine slathered on super-bland white bread, covered by a couple slices of—can I say the V word?—V------a, ahem, processed cheese, and pan-roasted or toasted till it was dark brown. This is my upgrade with pungent Gorgonzola leading the way, and creamy Taleggio taming some of the tang of the Gorgonzola. But my secret weapon here is the red onion jam, which brings a special dash to this sandwich. Once you taste it, I think you may want to start putting it on everything. Take the time to properly butter the outside of the crusty artisanal bread, and I am confident that you'll have mouthfuls of crunchy, melty goodnessness (more goodness than one word can hold!).

SERVES 4

RED ONION JAM:

3 tablespoons olive oil

1 large red onion, sliced

3 tablespoons light brown sugar

¼ cup red wine vinegar

GRILLED CHEESE SANDWICHES:

4 tablespoons butter, softened

1 loaf crusty, rustic Italian bread, cut into 8 slices

½ pound Taleggio cheese, cut into 8 slices

¼ pound Gorgonzola, cut into 4 slices

RED ONION JAM:

1. Heat the olive oil in a large skillet over medium-low heat. Add the onions and cook until soft and translucent, about 10 to 15 minutes.

2. Add the sugar, red wine vinegar, and 3 tablespoons water and cook until the liquid is reduced completely and the onions are caramelized, about 10 minutes. Set aside.

GRILLED CHEESE SANDWICHES:

1. Butter the outside of each slice of bread and arrange half of them, butter-side down, on a sheet pan.

2. Put 1 piece of Taleggio cheese onto a slice of the buttered bread, then top with a piece of Gorgonzola. Top with a heaping tablespoon of the onion jam and another slice of the Taleggio. Cover with a slice of bread, buttered side out. Repeat with the remaining ingredients.

3. Heat a large skillet over medium-low heat. Put the sandwiches in the skillet and cook until the bread is toasted and golden and the cheeses are melted, about 4 minutes per side. Slice each sandwich in half and serve.

MISSED PUTT PIZZA

Making this pizza has become a holiday tradition with my nephews and nieces. They crowd into my kitchen, taking turns rolling out the dough and topping it with all their favorite ingredients. My niece Laura has to have green chile and pineapple together. Nephew Nate wants BBQ chicken with grilled onions. My niece Keli is just like her uncle and likes arugula and prosciutto, while her sister Ashley wants all meat—taco meat, pepperoni, sausage, and so on. And I don't have enough room to list the eleven things that Natalie wants.

It is just so easy to make this pizza crust. I keep the crust extra crunchy and golden brown with a quick brush of olive oil before it goes in the oven. The key to sliding the pizza off the pizza paddle is dusting the paddle with cornmeal, which acts like little ball bearings. Keep in mind you can mix it up. The crust and sauce can be used for your own favorite play of flavors.

MAKES 2 PIZZAS, SERVES 4

DOUGH:

½ teaspoon sugar

1 teaspoon active dry yeast

3¾ cups all-purpose flour, plus ¼ cup
    for rolling out the dough

1 teaspoon salt

1 tablespoon olive oil, divided

DOUGH:

1. Combine 1¼ cups warm water with the sugar and yeast in the bowl of a standing mixer fitted with a dough hook. Let sit for 5 minutes, or until the yeast begins to bloom. The water will get foamy and bubbly when it's ready.

2. Add the flour, salt, and 1 tablespoon of olive oil. Mix on medium speed until the dough is smooth, soft, and stretchy, about 5 to 7 minutes.

3. Remove the bowl from the mixer and cover it with a damp towel or plastic wrap. Put it in a warm spot until the dough has doubled in volume, about 1½ hours.

4. Punch the dough down and remove it from the bowl. Divide the dough into 2 equal portions and roll each into a ball.

5. Place the balls on a floured cutting board, dust the dough with flour, and cover with a kitchen towel or plastic wrap. Let sit in warm spot for another 1½ hours.

SAUCE:

3 tablespoons olive oil

1 small yellow onion, diced

4 small cloves garlic, chopped

½ teaspoon red pepper flakes

1 teaspoon dried oregano

1 (28-ounce) can crushed tomatoes

4 basil leaves, sliced

Salt and freshly ground black pepper
   to taste

SAUCE:

1. Heat the olive oil in a medium saucepan over medium heat. Add the onion and sauté until soft and translucent, about 3 minutes.

2. Add the garlic, red pepper flakes, and oregano and sauté for another 2 minutes. Stir in the crushed tomatoes and basil.

3. Season with salt and pepper to taste, and simmer for 10 to 15 minutes over low heat. Remove from the heat and let cool to room temperature.

TOPPINGS AND BUILDING THE PIZZA:

¼ pound pancetta, diced

3 medium yellow onions, sliced thin

1 roasted red pepper, cut into strips

¼ cup cornmeal, for dusting

4 tablespoons olive oil

8 ounces whole-milk mozzarella
   cheese, sliced into thin rounds

BRIAN'S KITCHEN POINTER

Many years ago I made a great investment—a pizza stone. A pizza stone gets super hot and dispenses heat evenly under the bottom of the pizza. It also pulls moisture from the dough, so it gives your pizza that Italian wood-fired oven crunch. If you can't get to the store before you make your pizza tonight, use an upside-down sheet pan instead.

TOPPINGS:

1. Cook the pancetta in a large skillet over medium heat until it's brown and crispy. Remove and place on a plate lined with a paper towel.

2. Add the onions to the pan in which you cooked the pancetta. Lower the heat to medium-low.

3. Cook the onions until golden brown and caramelized, making sure to stir every few minutes for about 25 minutes. Remove the onions to a plate and set aside.

BUILDING THE PIZZA:

1. Line an outdoor grill with clay bricks, and place a pizza stone on top of the bricks. Cover, turn the grill on high, and heat to 500°F. Allow the grill to heat for 30 minutes so the bricks and pizza stone can come to temperature. (You can cook the pizza in an oven by placing the pizza stone on a rack in the middle of the oven and preheating the oven to 500°F.)

2. Roll out one ball of dough into a 12-inch round on a floured work surface.

3. Cover a pizza paddle or the backside of a sheet pan with 2 tablespoons of the cornmeal. Put the dough on the paddle. Brush the dough with 2 tablespoons of olive oil.

4. Spread half of the sauce evenly over the dough, leaving a 1-inch space between the edge of the sauce and outer edge of the dough. Top with half of the cheese and half of all of the toppings.

5. Carefully slide the pizza off of the paddle or sheet pan onto the hot pizza stone. Cover and cook until the crust is brown and cheese is melted and bubbly, about 10 minutes.

6. Remove the pizza from the grill or oven, slice, and serve hot.

7. Repeat step 4 with the remaining dough and toppings.

TANTALIZING SOUPS

I came across one of the best soups I've ever tasted at a dinner I attended recently filled with fresh, foraged ingredients. My friend Mitch invited me to his San Francisco restaurant Salt House for the dinner in honor of Connie Green, who is a forager. I'm a wannabe one, and have been ever since sixth grade. Back then, every kid in my part of the Bay Area went through the same rite of passage between elementary and junior high school: a weeklong camping trip to Redwood Glen, a sleepaway camp in the depths of the Santa Cruz mountains.

Part of the camping experience was survival training. (I know it sounds funny for sixth-graders to be learning about wilderness survival.) We were taken on foraging hunts accompanied by guides to identify plants that could be eaten. Before the week's end, we were asked to go find the same plants ourselves and create a chart with the dried leaves we'd gathered. At the time I thought it was all pretty interesting, and truth be told, I still do. I still have that chart somewhere.

Anyway, back to that delicious soup. The first course: English pea soup with leek and nettle ravioli. The peas were the freshest I've ever had, with a lightly sweet, grassy taste that blended perfectly with the subtle onion flavor of the leeks. The soup had so much flavor, it was what early spring would taste like pureed and put in a bowl!

That soup and its super-fresh ingredients were in the back of my mind as I developed the recipes that follow. They can make wholesome, nutritional meals with unexpected combinations of flavors, like the hot sausage and smooth cannellini beans in the Spicy Sausage Soup with Cannellini Beans and Escarole on page 56. Even if you don't forage for your soup ingredients, the flavors in these soups will provide a savory adventure of discovery.

BUTTERNUT SQUASH SOUP *with* GOAT CHEESE TOASTS

I first made this soup for my mom—she has a little bit of a (actually closer to a big) sweet tooth, and I found that this recipe is so easy to fine-tune for just about any preference. When I make it for my mom, I roast the squash with brown sugar and blend in half a ripe pear or apple to sweeten it and add another layer of flavor. Whether you make it sweeter or less sweet, the fresh squash flavor comes through, making for a full-bodied soup with a touch of spicy creaminess. The goat cheese–slathered toasts provide some contrast and a gratifying crunch.

SERVES 4

1 small butternut squash

6 tablespoons olive oil, divided

Salt and freshly ground black pepper to taste

1 mini French baguette

1 medium yellow onion, sliced

2 cloves garlic, chopped

1 quart vegetable broth

¼ teaspoon cayenne pepper

Juice of 1 lemon

1 tablespoon balsamic vinegar

1 (4-ounce) log goat cheese, softened

BRIAN'S KITCHEN POINTER

When making soups, you can always cook up an extra-big batch and freeze whatever is left over. Just put individual servings of the soup in resealable containers and pop them into the freezer. That way, whenever you feel like a bowl of soup, you can just warm it up, and it tastes even better when you don't have to prepare it again. This works with any soup in this chapter.

1. Preheat the oven to 400°F.

2. Slice the squash in half lengthwise and remove the seeds with a spoon. Coat the cut side of each half with 1 tablespoon of olive oil and season with salt and pepper. Place each half cut-side down on a baking sheet and roast for about 1 hour, or until the flesh is tender.

3. Remove the squash from the oven and let it sit until cool enough to handle but still warm. Scoop out the flesh with a spoon, place in a medium bowl, and set aside. Discard the skin.

4. Slice the bread into ¼-inch slices. Place them on a sheet pan fitted with a rack and brush each slice with a bit of olive oil. Toast in the oven for about 8 minutes, or until crisp. Set aside.

5. Add the remaining olive oil to a large pot over medium heat. Add the onions, season with a pinch of salt, and sauté until the onions are translucent and tender, about 10 minutes. Add the garlic and sauté for another 2 minutes.

6. Add the squash flesh to the pot, along with 2 cups of the broth. Simmer for about 2 minutes.

7. Puree the ingredients in the pot with an immersion blender until smooth. (If you do not have an immersion blender, combine the onions and squash and 2 cups of vegetable broth in a food processor fitted with the blade attachment, or in a blender. Puree until smooth, and return to the pot.)

8. Blend in the remaining broth, cayenne, lemon juice, and balsamic vinegar (using the immersion blender or use a food processor or blender), and add salt and pepper to taste. Let simmer for 5 minutes.

9. Spread the goat cheese on the toasted bread slices. Ladle the soup into bowls and serve with goat cheese toast on the side.

SPICY SAUSAGE SOUP *with* CANNELLINI BEANS *and* ESCAROLE

Katarina Witt, Dorothy Hamill, and I decided to rent a bus together one year when we were touring with Champions on Ice. After years of traveling and getting on flights every day, we were tired of packing and unpacking and basically schlepping everywhere. The bus allowed us to travel and sleep through the night and wake up at the next arena. Our bus driver, Earl, made a different soup or stew for us every night. It was waiting for us steaming hot when we got on board, and was just the touch of home we needed to handle months on the road.

There's a fine line between soup and stew, and this dish rests right on that line. The cannellini beans are often called "white kidney beans," and they have a creamy and slightly nutty taste that makes them a regular in all kinds of Italian dishes and in my kitchen. This soup is also versatile. You can make it vegetarian by simply omitting the sausage. Either way, this soup qualifies as a full-scale meal in a bowl. If you can't find escarole, you can substitute kale or spinach.

SERVES 4

3 tablespoons olive oil

1 pound spicy Italian chicken sausage, removed from casing

1 large yellow onion, diced

Salt and freshly ground black pepper to taste

1 red bell pepper, seeded and sliced

3 cloves garlic, chopped

¼ teaspoon red pepper flakes

6 cups vegetable broth

1 tablespoon red wine vinegar

2 (15-ounce) cans cannellini beans, rinsed and drained

1 head escarole, washed and chopped coarse

½ teaspoon dried oregano

1. Heat the olive oil in a large pot over medium-high heat. Break the sausage into pieces and add it to the pot. Cook until brown and cooked through, about 6 minutes. Remove with a slotted spoon to a plate.

2. Add the onions to the pot and reduce the heat to medium. Season with salt and pepper and cook until the onions are tender, about 5 minutes.

3. Add the bell pepper, garlic, and red pepper flakes to the pot and cook for four minutes.

4. Add the broth and bring to a simmer. Add the cooked sausage and remaining ingredients to the pot and simmer for 5 minutes before serving.

SWEET CORN CHOWDER

I grew up on the famous clam chowders of Fisherman's Wharf in San Francisco, but I've since fallen in love with corn chowder. It is, to my mind, one of the most delicious chowders you can make. This version is bold on the spice, so dial it down if the heat is too much for your palate. The sweetness of the corn and the smooth potato base are what make this a go-to comfort food for me. It's a truly summery mix of flavors, but at the same time hearty enough for winter.

SERVES 4

¼ cup olive oil

2 medium yellow onions, diced

Salt

2 cloves garlic, chopped

½ teaspoon red pepper flakes

¼ cup all-purpose flour

1 quart chicken broth

3 red potatoes, diced

Freshly ground black pepper to taste

4 ears of corn, kernels removed and cobs reserved

½ teaspoon smoked paprika, plus more for garnish

2 teaspoons fresh thyme

1 tablespoon chopped fresh parsley

2 cups whole milk

4 teaspoons avocado oil, for garnish

1. Heat the olive oil in a large saucepot over medium heat. Add the onions, season with a bit of salt, and sauté for 5 minutes, or until softened.

2. Add the garlic and red pepper flakes to the saucepan and sauté for 1 minute. Add the flour and cook for an additional 3 minutes, stirring constantly.

3. Whisk in the broth and add the potatoes; season with salt and pepper and simmer for about 8 minutes until the potatoes start to become tender.

4. Add the remaining ingredients up to and including the milk, including the corn kernels and corn cobs, and simmer for 5 minutes.

5. Ladle 2 cups of the soup into a blender and puree until smooth. Return to the saucepan. Taste and season with more salt and pepper as desired.

6. Simmer an additional 3 minutes. Remove the corn cobs and pour the soup into bowls. Garnish each bowl with a drizzle of avocado oil and a sprinkle of paprika.

SALADS

I USED TO EAT THE MOST BORING SALADS WHEN I WAS TRAINING. They generally consisted of iceberg lettuce with some pasta and sometimes included protein. I often topped them off with some diet blue cheese dressing. Yuck, right? Since then, I've come to appreciate just how satisfying salads can be with a little creativity and a lot more flavor. They are nutritious and are easy to prepare for people on the go. The recipes in this chapter are divided into two natural categories—light versus substantial—but keep in mind that lighter salads can easily be turned into stand-alone meals with the addition of the right protein. For instance, a citrusy salad like the Arugula and Nectarine Salad with Pepperoncini Vinaigrette and Olive Bread Croutons on page 71 would be the ideal base for tasty grilled prawns.

HEARTY MEAL-IN-ONE SALADS

Meal-in-one salads are a healthy obsession I trace all the way back to a summer I spent in Janesville, Wisconsin, when I was about twenty years old. I had traveled there to train with a group of other young skaters. My friend Annie and I saw our chance for a little downtime and some fun when we heard that ESPN would be covering the IROC races in nearby Elkhart Lake. Paul Newman was going to be racing, and we knew several people on the ESPN crew. Soon we found ourselves en route to Elkhart Lake and running low on gas. We pulled over at a truck stop to refuel and realized we were starving. But there were no restaurants for miles, so we grabbed dinner there.

Now, truck stop food is, well, truck stop food. The thing that I remember most about that truck stop is the steak salad I ordered at the diner. Their particular version was surprisingly one of the best salads I've ever eaten. The salad dressing was slightly creamy and the perfect complement of sweet and tangy. The meat was so tender you could almost cut it with a fork.

BRIAN'S KITCHEN POINTER

Preparing great salads also means concocting tasty dressings. You can use lots of different oils to make salad dressings. I've become particularly fond of avocado oil. Experts are calling it "the new olive oil" for its exceptional flavor and incredible health benefits. Avocado oil is filthy rich with omega-3 fatty acids that help improve heart health, as well vitamins E, A, and D. You can also use it as an accent in many recipes. You'll find it drizzled over my Sweet Corn Chowder (page 58), and it would be delicious on the Southwestern Sopapillas (page 10) or as an accent to add a slightly more exotic flavor to fish or seafood, such as Seared Halibut (page 155) or Shrimp and Polenta (page 152). It has a mild and distinctive taste, and basically you can use it in any dish calling for olive oil.

When all of the individual ingredients are done well, steak salad can't be beaten, offering all the flavors in one bite. It was unbelievable—especially since I never imagined finding such a delicious salad at a truck stop. I may never go back to Elkhart Lake or even back to Janesville, but if I do, I guarantee you I'll find my way back to that truck stop.

SAUTÉED VEGETABLE, CHICKEN, *and* QUINOA SALAD

People are always intrigued by quinoa. It provides a light base to the salad, adding an understated, nutty flavor that blends well with the rest of the flavors. And the red pepper brings a little fire to the simple chicken breast and grain. This dish is perfect for parties because it's easy to make large quantities—and you can give out a door prize for the first guest who pronounces it correctly. You can also make this into a vegetarian side dish by eliminating the chicken. If you are skeptical about the quinoa, try substituting brown rice or lentils.

SERVES 4

2 boneless, skinless chicken breasts

8 tablespoons olive oil, divided

Salt and freshly ground black pepper to taste

1 medium yellow onion, diced

1 red bell pepper, cored, seeded, and diced

1 large zucchini, sliced into half-moons

1 tablespoon white wine vinegar

¼ teaspoon red pepper flakes

1 clove garlic, chopped

3 cups cooked quinoa (prepared according to package instructions)

¼ cup chopped fresh Italian flat-leaf parsley

1. Preheat the oven to 350°F.

2. Coat the chicken breasts with 2 tablespoons olive oil. Season with salt and pepper and place on a baking sheet. Roast in the oven until cooked through, about 25 minutes. Let cool and dice.

3. Heat 2 tablespoons olive oil in a large skillet over medium-high heat. Add onions and bell peppers to the skillet. Season with salt and pepper to taste and sauté for 3 to 4 minutes, or until slightly tender.

4. Remove the onion and peppers to a plate and add 1 tablespoon olive oil to the skillet. Add the zucchini, and salt and pepper to taste. Sauté for 4 minutes, or until lightly browned on both sides. Remove to the plate with the peppers and onions.

5. In a large bowl, whisk together the remaining 3 tablespoons of olive oil, the white wine vinegar, red pepper flakes, and garlic.

6. Add the roasted chicken, sautéed vegetables, quinoa, and parsley to the bowl. Season with salt and pepper to taste, and toss to coat.

GRILLED CORN, JICAMA, *and* BEAN SALAD

My brother Mark lives in New Mexico, so he is heavily into Southwestern cuisine. His wife, Cory, loves to cook, and she is actually the one who introduced me to jicama years ago. Since then, I've been using it on a regular basis for many different recipes. Jicama is the centerpiece of this spicy Southwestern salad, bringing its characteristic juiciness and crunchy snap. The sweet grilled corn brings a lightly charred, smoky flavor that is enhanced by the citrus tang of the lime juice and cactus nectar. Feel free to up the amount of chili powder or hot sauce if you like your salad hotter.

SERVES 4

4 ears of corn, shucked

4 tablespoons canola oil, divided

Salt and freshly ground black pepper to taste

1 small jicama root

Juice of 2 limes

1 teaspoon agave nectar

½ teaspoon chili powder

1 teaspoon hot sauce

1 (15-ounce) can red beans, rinsed

1 (15-ounce) can black beans, rinsed

1 clove garlic, chopped

1. Preheat the grill on medium heat.

2. Brush the ears of corn with 1 tablespoon canola oil. Season each with salt and pepper. Grill for 12 minutes, until lightly charred, turning a quarter turn every 3 minutes.

3. Set the corn aside until it's cool enough to handle, about 5 minutes. Cut the kernels off each cob and discard the cobs.

4. Remove the jicama's skin with a knife. Slice the jicama in half, then slice each half in half again. Slice each quarter into ¼-inch pieces. Set aside.

5. In a large bowl, whisk 3 tablespoons canola oil with the lime juice, agave nectar, chili powder, and hot sauce.

6. Add the remaining ingredients, season with salt and pepper to taste, and toss to coat. Serve with a mariachi band playing in the background.

SUN-DRIED TOMATO CHICKEN SALAD

One of my favorite things about experimenting in the kitchen is putting a unique, contemporary spin on a traditional recipe. This version of the all-time deli standard, chicken salad, uses fresh ingredients that give the salad some crunch. You'll find two different dressings described in this recipe. The lighter one is oil-based, with a fresh finish and a bit more bite. The creamy dressing is a sweeter, thicker, more traditional option. Whichever you choose, eat this salad as a filling meal over salad greens, or make a delicious sandwich using crusty bread, pita, or a whole-wheat wrap, accompanied by a leaf of romaine lettuce and a couple slices of plum tomato. Or, like me, just eat it out of the bowl!

SERVES 2

2 boneless, skinless chicken breasts

Olive oil to coat chicken

Salt and freshly ground black pepper to taste

10 oil-packed sun-dried tomatoes, drained and chopped, reserve oil

1 tablespoon chopped fresh dill

1 shallot, diced

1 small orange bell pepper, seeded and diced

½ teaspoon celery seeds

½ teaspoon Worcestershire sauce

LIGHT DRESSING:

2 tablespoons olive oil

1 tablespoon oil from the sun-dried tomatoes

1 tablespoon white wine vinegar

1 tablespoon Dijon mustard

2 teaspoons juice from a jar of green olives

1 teaspoon honey

CREAMY DRESSING:

3 tablespoons canola oil mayonnaise

2 tablespoons Greek yogurt

1 tablespoon whole-grain mustard

2 teaspoons juice from a jar of green olives

1 teaspoon honey

1. Preheat the oven to 350°F.

2. Coat the chicken breasts with olive oil. Season each with a sprinkling of salt and pepper and place on a baking sheet. Roast in the oven until cooked through, about 25 minutes. Remove, allow chicken to cool, and dice.

3. Combine the diced chicken and remaining salad ingredients in a large bowl.

4. In a medium bowl, combine the ingredients for the dressing you prefer. Whisk until well blended.

5. Add the dressing to the chicken salad. Taste, and add salt and pepper as desired.

STEAK SALAD *with* GINGER DRESSING

Yep, that diner salad from the truck stop was good, but here is my upgrade. The snap peas add a crunchy texture that complements the greens and the steak nicely. When snap peas aren't available, you can use snow peas. The ginger dressing really pulls it all together. The miso paste in the dressing is made from fermented soybeans and is an essential ingredient in Japanese cooking. You can find it in Asian food stores. It's salty and the Japanese use miso because it adds so many layers of flavor. If you make the ginger dressing ahead of time, you can put this dinner together in the time it takes to prepare the steak.

SERVES 2

SALAD:

1 strip steak (about ¾ pound)

Salt and freshly ground black pepper to taste

6 cups mixed salad greens

1 cup sugar snap peas

1½ carrots, peeled and shredded

3 scallions, sliced

1 cup grape tomatoes, sliced in half

GINGER DRESSING:

½ carrot, peeled and chopped

1 tablespoon chopped fresh ginger

2 scallions, sliced

1 clove garlic

1 tablespoon white miso paste

1 tablespoon Dijon mustard

1 tablespoon soy sauce

2 tablespoons rice wine vinegar

3 tablespoons canola oil

1 teaspoon sesame oil

1. Preheat a grill pan over medium-high heat.

2. Generously season both sides of the steak with salt and pepper. Grill for about 4 minutes per side for medium-rare. Let rest for 10 minutes before slicing.

3. Combine the mixed greens, peas, carrots, scallions, and tomatoes in a large salad bowl.

4. Place all the dressing ingredients into a blender. Blend on medium speed until smooth. If the dressing is too thick, slowly add water while blending until it reaches the desired consistency.

5. Add three-quarters of the ginger dressing to the salad mix in the bowl and toss the salad. Divide the salad between 2 serving bowls. Top with the sliced steak and drizzle the remaining dressing over the top.

LIGHT & LIVELY

Las Vegas is probably the last place you would expect to
find a stunningly inventive, light, simple, and sparkling
fresh salad. (Well, maybe second-to-last place—see the
truck stop story on pages 62-63.) It is, after all, practically
the birthplace of the all-you-can-eat buffets that my
parents love. But that's exactly what happened the last
time I visited Vegas.

I was in town for a very secret meeting (what
happens in Vegas). OK, I was judging a television
culinary competition. There's a lot to see in Las Vegas,
but I was mostly interested in the recent explosion of
high-end restaurants.

I stayed at The Cosmopolitan, a swanky hotel
that sits right on the Vegas Strip with a collection
of incredible restaurants inside. There are so many
remarkable places to eat that I had a hard time picking
one, but in the end I made a night of it at chef José
Andres's Jaleo. It turned out to be a smart decision.

Jaleo is a celebration of Spanish culinary style, a
stunning restaurant with bright fuchsia stools set at high
wooden tables, under an orange-tiled ceiling. As fabulous
and colorful as the setting might be, Jaleo is most famous
for its chef and its menu of innovative tapas.

I don't usually think of salads when I think of tapas,
but I just had to try the warm sugar snap peas with
apricots, apple, and Serrano ham. Simple, but a total
knockout. It served as an inspiration for me to write a
couple of salad recipes using fresh fruit. Here are my
versions of some crunchy, salty, and spicy salads with
plenty of sweet fruit: Heirloom Tomato, Cantaloupe, and
Feta Salad (page 75) and Arugula and Nectarine Salad
with Pepperoncini Vinaigrette and Olive Bread Croutons
(opposite).

ARUGULA *and* NECTARINE SALAD *with* PEPPERONCINI VINAIGRETTE *and* OLIVE BREAD CROUTONS

I almost think of the salad in this recipe as a stage for the real star—the crunchy, delicious croutons. The combination of sweet nectarines and spiciness from the arugula and pepperoncini is a great co-star. I like serving this to friends for a casual brunch on my roof deck, with the umbrella up and the sun shining—especially with a nice, crisp Sauvignon Blanc. And don't worry if you can't find real olive bread: Use ciabatta or a similar crusty, artisan bread, and toss an extra ¼ cup of pitted kalamata olives into the salad to compensate for the missing olives in the bread. You can make extra dressing, store it in the refrigerator, and use it on salads for the next couple of weeks.

SERVES 4

CROUTONS:

⅓ loaf olive bread, cubed (about 2 cups)

3 tablespoons extra-virgin olive oil

VINAIGRETTE:

2 pickled pepperoncini, finely diced

3 tablespoons white wine vinegar

2 teaspoons honey

¼ teaspoon dried thyme (or 1 teaspoon fresh thyme)

⅓ cup extra-virgin olive oil

Salt and freshly ground black pepper to taste

1. Preheat the oven to 375°F.

2. Toss the bread cubes in a small bowl with the olive oil until coated. Spread them on a baking sheet in a single layer. Toast in the oven for 12 to 15 minutes, or until golden and crispy. Remove from the oven and set aside to cool.

3. Whisk together the diced pepperoncini, white wine vinegar, honey, and thyme in a small bowl. Slowly drizzle in olive oil while whisking, until the vinaigrette is completely blended together. Season with salt and pepper to taste.

BRIAN'S KITCHEN POINTER

Make this, or any citrus-based salad, into a protein-packed meal by adding grilled shrimp. Toss 1½ pounds of cleaned large shrimp in a bowl with ¼ cup of olive oil, the juice of 1 lemon, and a pinch of salt and pepper. Let the shrimp sit for 5 minutes, then grill them over medium-high heat for about 2 to 3 minutes per side. Let them cool slightly before placing them on top of the salad.

8 cups baby arugula

2 cups shaved fennel (use a
     mandoline)

2 yellow nectarines, peeled, pits
     removed, and sliced

½ cup pitted kalamata olives, halved

Salt and freshly ground black pepper
     to taste

4. In a large bowl, gently toss the arugula with the fennel, nectarine slices, olives, and half the croutons.

5. Slowly pour the vinaigrette over the salad and toss until all the ingredients are evenly coated. Season with salt and pepper, as desired.

6. Transfer the salad to a serving platter or bowl, and top with the remaining croutons before serving.

BRIAN'S KITCHEN POINTER

If nectarines are out of season or if you just can't find them locally, you can substitute oranges. They will work just as well with the other flavors in this salad. And whenever you're using fresh citrus in a salad recipe, try cutting them into supremes. Supremes are segments of the pure flesh of the fruit, without the bitter rind, membrane, or stringy remnants of the peel. First, cut off just enough of the ends of the fruit to reveal the tops and bottoms of the individual segments. Sit the citrus with one end on the counter, and use a paring knife to carefully cut away the rind, following the curve of the fruit. The idea is to entirely remove the bitter white layer while leaving the juicy flesh. The lines of the membranes separating the sections should be clearly visible. Now cut down along the inside edges on each side of each membrane, separating out a wedge of pure citrus flesh. Cut carefully and you'll have attractive citrus supremes full of flavor—and nothing else.

HEIRLOOM TOMATO, CANTALOUPE, *and* FETA SALAD

I created this salad from ingredients I had on hand one night when I was craving something a little unusual and refreshing, and I didn't feel like going to the grocery store. There are just a few ingredients, and it's so easy to prepare. The balsamic vinegar accents and emphasizes the sweetness of the cantaloupe, and the feta naturally complements both. Roasted pine nuts bring some smoky-flavored crunch.

SERVES 4

½ cup pine nuts

3 tablespoons avocado oil

1½ tablespoons white balsamic vinegar

2 cups diced (2-inch cubes) cantaloupe

2 heirloom tomatoes, diced

1 cup crumbled feta cheese

10 basil leaves, torn into coarse pieces

Salt and freshly ground black pepper to taste

1. Place the pine nuts in a large skillet over medium-low heat. Toast for 5 minutes, or until lightly browned, tossing frequently. Let cool.

2. Whisk together the avocado oil and balsamic vinegar in a large bowl.

3. Add the remaining ingredients and the toasted pine nuts to the bowl, and toss to coat.

BRIAN'S KITCHEN POINTER

Feel free to replace the feta with goat cheese and if you don't have avocado oil, olive oil works just as well.

CARROT *and* RED CABBAGE SLAW *with* CREAMY HERB DRESSING

Whenever I'm invited to a barbecue, my friends ask if I can make this slaw. It's a terrific dish to bring to a friend's house because it's so easy to make and the blend of colors looks really beautiful. The salad has a little bit of everything—a combination of crunchy, creamy, chewy, sweet, and tart.

SERVES 4

DRESSING:

¼ cup Greek yogurt

1 tablespoon mayonnaise

1 tablespoon crème fraîche

1 tablespoon honey

2 tablespoons white wine or champagne vinegar

2 tablespoons chopped fresh basil

2 tablespoons chopped fresh Italian flat-leaf parsley

2 tablespoons chopped fresh tarragon

SLAW:

½ head red cabbage, shredded

3 cups shredded carrots

4 scallions, sliced

¼ cup golden raisins

1 tablespoon poppy seeds

Salt and freshly ground black pepper to taste

1. Whisk together all the dressing ingredients in a large bowl.

2. Add all the slaw ingredients to the bowl. Toss thoroughly to combine.

3. Cover and refrigerate until ready to serve (at least 30 minutes, or as long as overnight, to let the flavors meld).

BRIAN'S KITCHEN POINTER

The best way to shred carrots and cabbage is with a mandoline. I find it to be an essential kitchen tool, perfect for shredding and thinly slicing vegetables. This salad is quick to make, but if you are looking to save even more time, you can always buy pre-shredded carrots and cabbage.

CUCUMBER *and* RADISH SALAD

I liked the spiciness of radishes even when I was little. I think it's because I had a small vegetable garden on the side of our house when I was ten years old, and I grew radishes from seeds. For some reason the radishes and pumpkins were the only things I could get to grow. I love serving them to this day—the radishes, not the pumpkins—to guests when they first arrive, just cleaned and whole with a bowl of sea salt to dunk them in. If you don't have brown rice syrup, you can always use honey or agave nectar as a substitute in this recipe.

SERVES 4

Juice of 1 lemon

3 tablespoons olive oil

1 teaspoon brown rice syrup

1 English cucumber, diced

1 bunch radishes, julienned

3 scallions, sliced

2 tablespoons plus 1 teaspoon
fresh thyme

Salt and freshly ground black pepper
to taste

1. In a large bowl, whisk together the lemon juice, olive oil, and brown rice syrup.

2. Add the remaining ingredients and toss to coat.

PASTA

EATING PASTA IS A PART OF THE BOITANO FAMILY TRADITIONS and is certainly a part of our heritage. There is still a small village in the Ligurian region of Italy full of Boitanos who rarely go a whole day without enjoying a plate of pasta. In fact, it was my grandma, who stood about five foot nothing, with an incredible smile and a fun-loving feistiness, who introduced me to the pleasures of well-made pasta.

When I was a little boy, my parents would herd us kids into the car every couple of weeks to make the drive to my nana's house in San Francisco. It was the coolest house, very old San Francisco in a funky but good way. There were lavender tiles in the bathroom, and a "rumpus" room with banquettes and a pool table and a U-shaped bar. But best of all was Nana's pasta.

I remember being amazed by her ravioli. I was a little kid, and each ravioli was almost the size of my small hand. She would fill the fresh pasta with spinach, ricotta, and whole pine nuts. Then, she'd carefully crimp the edges and layer the ravioli in a giant pot (more of a cauldron, really) with a big wooden handle. We'd eat them with her homemade marinara. My magic number was two. I could never eat more than that, even though I wanted to.

I think about her ravioli whenever I eat stuffed pasta. I would love to make Nana's ravioli (and include it in this book!) but, sadly, she never wrote down her recipe. She had learned how to make the ravioli at her mother's side and carried the recipe in her head. Lost treasures like Nana's ravioli are a big reason why I write down all my recipes.

Pasta is the ultimate comfort food, and it is so adaptable. There are hundreds of shapes and sizes of pastas in Italy, and more and more make their way to America all the time. No matter which you choose, properly made pasta grabs ahold of the sauce. It becomes the perfect vehicle for an amazing diversity of flavors, from deep, rich, and hearty to light, crisp, and refreshing.

LIGHT PASTA FOR NICE WEATHER

A few years ago I went to visit my great-grandparents' village of Favale di Malvaro, near Genoa, Italy. My family had emigrated to the United States from Favale in the late 1800s.

The people in my great-grandparents' hometown still live a slow village life, making what they need by hand and foraging for everything from porcini mushrooms to wild herbs. They make their own delicious bread, different types of the classic Italian liquor Limoncello, and some truly incredible warm-weather pastas. In fact, the Ligurian region itself is famous for—among many other things—inventing pesto. And doesn't everyone love pesto?

I don't know why, but pesto just tastes better when you eat it in Liguria, especially Genoa. My cousin Luciano in Favale told me that their local basil is grown in sandy soil on the banks of the river, and that's why it tastes so good. Who knows? All I know is that it is one of my favorite sauces, and I love to try different variations. You'll find my own version in the recipe for Spinach and Almond Pesto over Rotini, on page 94. Ligurians also eat a lot of seafood because the ocean is in their front yard. Fresh seafood pasta is perfect for hot weather and eating al fresco. My take— Linguine with Shrimp, Scallops, and Chorizo—is up next.

BRIAN'S KITCHEN POINTER

Guarantee yourself great pasta time after time by following a few basic rules. Always use a lot of water—probably more than you think necessary (follow the directions on the box)—and be sure to add a generous amount of salt to the water. Never use oil in the water; although it may keep the pasta from sticking to itself, it will also keep the sauce from sticking to the pasta. Pasta should be cooked al dente, with just a little resistance to your bite but still tender when you chew. To cook pasta al dente, test it frequently as it cooks. When the pasta is done, remove it immediately and drain—but don't rinse—it. Return it to the original pot with a cup or two of sauce, and toss to coat the noodles and saturate them with the flavors. Then add the rest of the sauce. Avoid the common mistake of using too much sauce. Use just enough to coat the noodles, but not so much that it pools in the serving dish.

LINGUINE *with* SHRIMP, SCALLOPS, *and* CHORIZO

This seafood pasta is inspired by my visits to Liguria, which is known for its steep terrain that plunges into the ocean. It's so steep that in the old days, people used to take boats to visit other villages because it was easier than walking along the hills. If you are going to Liguria, plan to eat a lot of fish. Make sure you use Spanish chorizo, not fresh Mexican chorizo, in this recipe. You can also use the Portuguese version of chorizo, linguiça.

SERVES 4

6 tablespoons olive oil, divided

½ pound cured chorizo, diced fine

2 shallots, diced fine

1½ cups white wine

2 tablespoons butter

¾ pound linguine

1 pound extra-large shrimp, shelled and deveined, patted dry

Salt and freshly ground black pepper to taste

1 pound (about 12 large) sea scallops, patted dry

Juice of ½ lemon

¼ cup chopped fresh parsley

1. Add 2 tablespoons of olive oil to a large skillet over medium heat. Add chorizo and cook for 2 minutes.

2. Add shallots and cook for 2 minutes until translucent. Add the white wine, turn the heat to medium-high, and bring to a simmer. Simmer until it reduces by three-quarters, or about 10 minutes.

3. When the liquid in the skillet is reduced, turn off the heat and stir in the butter. Transfer the contents of the skillet to a medium bowl.

4. Bring a large pot of generously salted water to a boil. Add the linguine and cook about 8 minutes, or until al dente.

5. Heat 2 tablespoons of olive oil in the skillet over medium-high heat.

6. Coat both sides of the shrimp with salt and pepper. Add the shrimp to the skillet and cook until they are pink and light brown on the edges, about 2 to 3 minutes per side. Remove the shrimp and add them to the chorizo mixture.

7. Season both sides of the scallops with salt and pepper. Add the remaining 2 tablespoons of olive oil to the skillet. Sear the scallops on both sides, about 3 to 4 minutes on the first side and 30 seconds on the second.

8. Turn the heat down to medium-low and add the shrimp-and-chorizo mixture to the skillet. Toss to coat.

9. Add the cooked and drained linguine, lemon juice, and parsley and toss to combine. Transfer to a serving bowl and serve immediately.

ARTICHOKE *and* SPINACH PASTA

I made this dish on the *Today* show—it's so simple and quick and also has the perfect ingredients for a light spring meal. I like to add spinach at the last minute so it's just lightly wilted. People often overlook fresh artichokes, but the truth is they taste so much better. This dish comes together super quickly if you prepare the artichokes the day before.

SERVES 4

4 large artichokes

4 whole cloves garlic, plus 1 clove chopped

Salt

5 tablespoons olive oil, divided

½ pound spaghetti

½ medium yellow onion, chopped

½ pint baby heirloom or grape tomatoes

½ lemon

½ cup vegetable or chicken broth

¼ cup dry white wine

Freshly ground black pepper to taste

6 basil leaves, chopped

1 tablespoon butter

1 (6-ounce) bag fresh baby spinach

1 cup grated Parmesan, plus a small block for ribbons

¼ cup chopped fresh chives, chopped

1. Preheat the oven to 425°F.

2. Use a serrated knife to cut 1 inch off the top and ½ inch off the stem of each artichoke.

3. Place each artichoke in the center of a large piece of aluminum foil. Push a clove of garlic down about an inch or so into the center of each artichoke.

4. Sprinkle each artichoke with salt and drizzle 2 tablespoons olive oil over the top. Gather up the corners of the foil and press together on top to tightly seal the artichoke. (You can wrap it in a second piece of foil if you don't think you have a tight-enough seal.)

5. Roast the artichokes in a roasting pan for 30 to 45 minutes, or until the stem is fork tender.

6. Let the artichokes cool down to room temperature. Peel the leaves off to get to the heart. Carefully clean the furry center out of each heart with a knife or spoon. Slice the hearts into strips about ¼ inch thick.

7. Bring 6 cups of salted water to a boil in a large pot. Add the spaghetti to the boiling water and cook for about 7 minutes, or until al dente.

8. Heat 2 tablespoons of olive oil in a large skillet over medium heat. Sauté the onion until translucent, about 5 minutes.

9. Add the chopped garlic and sauté for another minute. Add the tomatoes, juice from ½ lemon, vegetable broth, white wine, and salt and pepper to taste. Simmer for 5 minutes.

10. Add the artichoke hearts to the skillet and gently toss, being careful not to stir the hearts too much because they may fall apart. If the mixture looks too dry, add a little more broth. Add the basil and butter to the mixture.

11. When the pasta is cooked, drain it and return it to the pot. Add the tomato-artichoke mixture to the pot, along with the fresh spinach and grated Parmesan. Mix thoroughly, taste, and adjust seasoning if necessary.

12. Serve in a large bowl or plate. Garnish with ribbons of Parmesan, chives, and drizzle with the 1 tablespoon of remaining olive oil.

SUMMER SQUASH RISOTTO
with GRILLED LEMON BASIL CHICKEN

This dish is both nutritious and delicious. Summer squash is crammed with protein, fiber, vitamins C and B_1, and beta carotene, and the grilled chicken is a healthy low-fat alternative to red meat. Arborio rice is plumper than normal rice and gives off a lot of starch, which in turn makes the risotto creamy. Also, because the grains are large, they are able to absorb all the summery flavors in this dish.

SERVES 4

2 boneless, skinless chicken breasts, sliced in half lengthwise

Salt and freshly ground black pepper to taste

½ cup olive oil, divided

2 cloves garlic, chopped

Juice and zest of 1 lemon

12 basil leaves, chopped, plus 8 whole leaves for garnish

1 large yellow squash

1 medium zucchini

1 medium yellow onion, diced

1½ cups arborio rice

1½ cups dry white wine

5 cups chicken broth

¼ cup grated Parmesan

BRIAN'S KITCHEN POINTER

The lemon basil chicken breasts in this recipe can be used in lots of other ways. Make more than you need, then use them for great-tasting sandwiches the next day, or go for the lighter option of chicken served between two lettuce leaves.

1. Place the chicken breasts in a small baking dish and season both sides of each breast with salt and pepper.

2. Whisk ¼ cup of olive oil with the garlic, lemon juice, and chopped basil leaves in a small bowl. Pour the mixture over the chicken breasts, making sure to coat the chicken completely. Cover the dish with plastic wrap and chill in the refrigerator for at least 30 minutes, or up to 2 hours.

3. Preheat the grill to medium heat.

4. Cut the stem ends off the squash and zucchini, and slice in half lengthwise. Coat each half with olive oil, using 2 tablespoons total, and season with salt and pepper.

5. Remove the chicken from the marinade and drain off any excess. Grill until cooked through, 3 to 4 minutes per side. Remove and let rest for 5 minutes. Slice into strips.

6. Grill the squash and zucchini until seared with grill marks and slightly tender, about 2 to 3 minutes per side. Remove and let cool. Slice into ½-inch-thick half-moons.

7. Heat 2 tablespoons of olive oil in a large high-sided skillet over medium heat. Add the onion, season with salt and pepper, and cook for about 5 minutes, or until the onion is translucent and tender.

8. Add the rice and cook for 3 minutes more, or until the rice is lightly toasted, stirring occasionally. Add 1 cup of white wine and cook, stirring constantly until almost all of the wine has been absorbed and the rice starts to become translucent.

9. Add the remaining ½ cup of wine and 1 cup of broth and stir until the liquid is mostly absorbed, about 5 to 7 minutes. Continue adding broth, ½ cup at a time, until the rice is tender but still slightly firm to the bite. The risotto should have a creamy yet pourable consistency. If it's too thick, add a small amount of broth.

10. Stir in the lemon zest, Parmesan, and half the grilled squash and zucchini. Add salt and pepper to taste.

11. Divide the risotto among 4 plates. Top each with the sliced chicken and remaining grilled squash and zucchini. Garnish with basil and serve immediately.

PENNE *with* BROCCOLI RABE *and* GOAT CHEESE

Every time I went to train in Toronto with my choreographer Sandra, her then husband, Dino, made a pasta dish with broccoli rabe. I just loved it. He called it by its Italian name, rapini, and I could never find it. Finally, I discovered rapini was just another name for broccoli rabe, and I ran right out and picked some up. This is my version of Dino's pasta. It balances the pleasantly bitter bite of the broccoli rabe against the creamy, mildly tangy nature of the goat cheese. If you're not a fan of goat cheese or are just looking to try something different, you can use ricotta instead.

SERVES 4

Salt

2 bunches (approximately 1 pound each) broccoli rabe

½ pound penne pasta

3 tablespoons olive oil

1 large yellow onion, sliced

Freshly ground black pepper to taste

4 cloves garlic, chopped

¼ teaspoon red pepper flakes

1 (6-ounce) log goat cheese, sliced into chunks

12 fresh basil leaves, chopped

1. Fill a large pot with 8 cups of water, add 2 tablespoons of salt, and bring the water to a boil.

2. Cut off 1 inch of the broccoli rabe stems and discard. Cut the bottom remaining portion including leaves, into 2-inch pieces.

3. Blanch the rabe in the boiling water for 1 minute. Remove to a colander (reserving the water) and run cold water over the rabe. Allow it to drain, then spread out the cut pieces on a sheet pan lined with paper towels to dry. Use a spider or slotted spoon to transfer the broccoli rabe to a bowl, and keep the hot salted water in the pot for the pasta.

4. Add penne to the pot and cook for about 10 minutes, or until al dente. Once the pasta is cooked, drain it in the colander, reserving 1 cup of the pasta water.

5. While the pasta is cooking, heat the olive oil in a large skillet over medium heat. Add the onions, season with salt and pepper, and cook for 5 minutes, or until the onions are translucent and tender.

6. Add the garlic and red pepper flakes and cook for about 1 minute.

7. Add the broccoli rabe to the skillet, season with salt and pepper, and cook until heated through, about 1 minute.

8. Return the pasta to the pot, along with the skillet mixture. Heat the pot on medium heat, and add the goat cheese and basil. Stir until the goat cheese begins to melt and forms a creamy sauce.

9. Add a small amount of the reserved pasta water if the sauce is too thick. Taste and add salt and pepper as desired. Transfer to a serving bowl and serve immediately.

SPINACH *and* ALMOND PESTO *over* ROTINI

All the pestos in Liguria, Italy, use mostly the same ingredients, but somehow they are all different. It seems like every restaurant has its own style. One restaurant will make it creamier and thicker, while the next one will make it lighter with just a little olive oil and the herbs chopped rather than blended. It's funny—every time you try a new one, you'd swear it was the best you've ever tasted. Here is my version of pesto, featuring almonds instead of pine nuts and spinach instead of basil. The flavor is simple and pleasing but with a good deal of salty bite.

SERVES 4

½ pound rotini pasta or cavatelli

¼ cup slivered almonds, toasted

1 anchovy (optional)

3 cloves garlic

Pinch of red pepper flakes

5 cups baby spinach

1 cup basil leaves

½ cup Italian flat-leaf parsley

⅓ cup finely grated Parmesan

Zest and juice of ½ lemon

⅓ cup extra-virgin olive oil

Salt and freshly ground black paper to taste

1. Cook the pasta according to package instructions. Drain and return to the pot.

2. While the pasta is cooking, add the almonds to a food processor fitted with the blade attachment. Pulse until the almonds are finely ground.

3. Add the anchovy, garlic, and red pepper flakes and pulse until the garlic is finely chopped.

4. Add the spinach, basil, parsley, Parmesan, lemon juice, and zest. With the processor running, slowly pour in the olive oil, blending until the mixture is smooth. Taste and add salt and pepper as desired. Pulse to incorporate.

5. Add all but 2 tablespoons of the pesto to the cooked pasta and toss to combine. Transfer to a serving bowl, garnish with the reserved 2 tablespoons of pesto, and serve.

BRIAN'S KITCHEN POINTER

Last time I was in Genoa, I had an incredible dish that I had never come across before. The restaurant served pesto with sheet pasta—6 x 6-inch uncut sheets of pasta. The sheets were tossed with the pesto and casually crumpled into a baking pan. To serve it, they cut it with a spatula. If you make your own pasta, save yourself a little effort and leave the sheet uncut. Then you can serve it in that rustic style with my spinach and almond pesto for a unique presentation.

A WINTER-WARMING PLATE OF PASTA

When I was preparing for the movie *Carmen on Ice,* I spent a month in Toronto working with my choreographer Sandra on hours and hours of choreography. Sandra and I worked every night alone on the ice, usually finishing at 3:00 or 4:00 in the morning. Building a professional ice-skating routine involves seemingly endless repetition and small adjustments, playing the music dozens of times a night. After long hours on the ice, I was totally stiff and fatigued, and I just wanted a warm meal and a comfortable place to relax.

Enter Sandra's then husband, Dino. Dino is Italian . . . can you tell by his name? And he could cook pasta like nobody's business. The only thing that kept me awake as Sandra and I drove home was the thought of Dino's cooking. We'd walk through the door into a garlic-scented cloud that was what Italian heaven must smell like. Dino made this incredible spaghetti Bolognese (rich and filling like the Coq au Vin-guine, page 100), and we'd just sit there for a couple hours winding down and eating wonderful pasta, accompanied by a glass of Amarone wine.

SPAGHETTI CARBONARA

There are all kinds of stories about where carbonara comes from, including the historical rumor that it was a filling meal favored by Italian coal miners, and the name actually derives from the Italian word for coal miner—carbonari. I had one of my favorite pasta carbonara dishes in a restaurant in Rome. It included butter for flavor, but I decided to keep it lighter in my recipe. The traditional pancetta makes this version just as tasty. The real key is knowing just when to add the eggs. If the pasta is hot, the eggs will scramble, so allow the pasta to cool a bit and the sauce will be creamier. Use a microplane to grate the Parmesan to ensure a smooth, creamy sauce.

SERVES 4

½ pound spaghetti

Salt

2 large eggs

½ cup grated Parmesan

¼ pound pancetta, diced

3 cloves garlic, chopped

2 tablespoons chopped parsley

Freshly ground black pepper to taste

1. Fill a large pot three-quarters full with well-salted water and bring to a boil. Add the spaghetti, stir, and cook until al dente, about 7 to 8 minutes. Drain the pasta, reserving 1 cup of the pasta water.

2. Whisk together the eggs and Parmesan in a medium bowl. Set aside.

3. Cook the pancetta in a large skillet over medium heat until brown and crispy. Remove to a plate lined with a paper towel.

4. Add the garlic to the skillet and cook for 1 minute. Turn off the heat and add the cooked spaghetti. Toss to coat.

5. Add the egg-and-cheese mixture to the skillet. Stir gently to coat the pasta and cook the eggs.

6. Add about ½ cup of the pasta water and continue to stir until the sauce thickens. If sauce is too thick, add more water. Mix in the pancetta. Salt and pepper, to taste.

7. Transfer to a serving bowl, top with the chopped parsley, and serve immediately.

COQ *au* VIN-GUINE

I made this pasta in an episode of my TV show when I was trying to get into my handyman Guy's supper club. When I made it, the cameramen kept sneaking bites behind my back. They especially loved the cipollini onions with their unusual, slightly sweet taste. One of the really great things about this dish is that you can make it using just one skillet. How can you not like limited cleanup?

SERVES 6

½ cup olive oil, divided

¼ pound pancetta, chopped

1 pound cipollini onions, peeled and sliced in half

½ cup all-purpose flour

Salt and freshly ground black pepper to taste

1½ pounds boneless, skinless chicken breast, cut into bite-size pieces

1 pound cremini mushrooms, sliced

2 cloves garlic, chopped

2 tablespoons tomato paste

1 (750-ml) bottle medium-bodied Italian red wine

3 sprigs fresh thyme, leaves removed

1 tablespoon unsalted butter

1 pound linguine

2 tablespoons coarsely chopped fresh parsley leaves

1. Heat 1 tablespoon of olive oil in a large skillet over medium heat. Add the pancetta and cook until brown and crispy, about 8 minutes. Remove with a slotted spoon to a plate lined with a paper towel.

2. Add the onions to the skillet and cook until they just begin to caramelize, about 10 minutes. Remove from the pan and set aside on a baking sheet.

3. While the onions are cooking, add the flour to a glass baking dish and season with salt and pepper. Add the chicken and toss to coat.

4. After removing the onions, add 3 tablespoons of olive oil to the skillet. Add the mushrooms and season with salt and pepper to taste. Sauté the mushrooms until browned, about 8 minutes. Remove to the baking sheet with the onions.

5. Shake any excess flour off of the chicken and put it on a plate. Add 3 tablespoons of olive oil to the skillet and add the chicken. Cook the chicken until browned, about 6 minutes. Transfer to the baking sheet.

6. Add the garlic and tomato paste to the skillet. Cook for 2 minutes, then deglaze the pan with three-quarters of the bottle of wine, making sure to scrape the brown bits from the bottom of the pan.

7. Add the thyme along with the chicken, mushrooms, and onions to the skillet and let simmer for 3 minutes. If the sauce is too thick, add the remaining wine. Add the butter, taste, and adjust the seasonings if necessary.

8. Bring a large pot three-quarters full of salted water to a boil over medium-high heat. Add the pasta and cook until al dente, about 8 to 10 minutes.

9. Drain the pasta, transfer to a large serving bowl, and top with the skillet sauce. Garnish with the parsley, pancetta, and a drizzle of the remaining olive oil.

RIGATONI *with* SPICY CHICKEN SAUSAGE, ASPARAGUS, EGGPLANT, *and* ROASTED PEPPERS

This is a good dish to serve when you are having both meat lovers and vegetarians over for dinner. Take out the sausage, and you have the perfect vegetarian pasta meal, with a spectacular medley of fresh vegetable flavors. You can satisfy meat eaters and vegetarians alike by cooking the sausage separately rather than using the same skillet as the vegetables, and then serving half the pasta with just the vegetables and the other half with the sausage.

SERVES 4

2 red bell peppers, sliced into strips

1 bunch asparagus

½ cup olive oil, divided

1 pound spicy Italian chicken sausage, removed from casing

½ pound rigatoni

1 baby eggplant, diced into ½-inch cubes

Salt and freshly ground black pepper to taste

3 cloves garlic, chopped

1 tablespoon red wine vinegar

¼ cup grated Parmesan

¼ cup chopped fresh parsley

1. Preheat the broiler, with the rack set about 6 inches under the broiler.

2. Place the peppers on a baking sheet under the broiler. Roast for about 8 to 10 minutes, turning a quarter turn every couple of minutes until charred on all sides.

3. Remove the peppers to a bowl and cover the bowl with plastic wrap. Let the peppers steam for 10 minutes.

4. Remove the peppers from the bowl and peel off the skins. You can use a paper towel to wipe off any small bits of skin. Carefully remove the cores and seeds, and reserve any liquid that has drained from the peppers. Slice into strips and set aside.

5. Bring a medium pot full of salted water to a boil. Cut the bottom 2 inches off of the asparagus stems and discard. Slice the asparagus into 1-inch pieces and blanch the pieces in the boiling water for 1 minute. Strain and rinse in cold water. Remove to a plate lined with a paper towel to dry.

6. Bring a large pot of salted water to a boil. While the water comes to a boil, heat 2 tablespoons of olive oil in a large skillet over medium-high heat.

7. Add the sausage to the skillet and, using a wooden spoon, break it up into small chunks. Cook for 6 to 8 minutes, stirring occasionally until cooked through. Remove to a plate.

8. Add the rigatoni to the boiling water and cook until al dente, about 10 minutes. Drain and add the pasta back to the pot.

BRIAN'S KITCHEN POINTER

You can also buy jarred peppers to save time. Simply slice into strips.

9. While the rigatoni is cooking, add 3 more tablespoons of olive oil to the skillet. Add the diced eggplant, season with salt and pepper, and cook for 5 to 6 minutes, or until brown and slightly tender.

10. Add 1 tablespoon of olive oil and the garlic to the skillet and cook for 1 minute. Add the roasted peppers, any reserved liquid from the peppers, the asparagus, sausage, and vinegar and cook for 2 minutes more.

11. Add the skillet mixture to the rigatoni in the pot. Add the Parmesan, parsley, and remaining 2 tablespoons of olive oil and stir to combine.

12. Taste and season with salt and pepper as desired. Transfer to a large bowl and serve immediately.

NOT YOUR MAMA'S SPAGHETTI *and* MEATBALLS

My mom's meatballs were one of my favorite meals growing up. She called her recipe "Porcupine Meatballs." It included adding rice to the meatball mix before cooking—a pretty interesting addition. When it came time to create my own meatballs, I went with an interesting mix as well: I included three types of meat that make for some wonderful flavor. Now my meatballs are my mom's favorite. Actually anything I cook is my mom's favorite. That's a mom for you.

You can change the meats to suit your own tastes, substituting veal for the lamb, for instance. To add more flavor to the sauce, deglaze the pan after the meatballs are cooked with ¼ cup water, scraping down the bits of browned meat from the pan and then adding the deglazing liquid to the sauce.

SERVES 6

MEATBALLS:

½ pound ground beef

½ pound ground pork

½ pound ground lamb

¾ cup bread crumbs

1 egg

¼ cup whole milk

1 teaspoon Italian seasoning

½ teaspoon garlic powder

½ cup grated Parmesan

1 tablespoon Worcestershire sauce

1 teaspoon salt

1 tablespoon freshly ground
    black pepper

3 tablespoons olive oil

SAUCE:

3 tablespoons olive oil

1 large yellow onion, diced

Salt and freshly ground black pepper
     to taste

1 (6-ounce) can tomato paste

5 cloves garlic, chopped

¼ teaspoon red pepper flakes

3 (28-ounce) cans whole plum
     tomatoes, crushed by hand

2 teaspoons sugar

1 teaspoon dried oregano

12 fresh basil leaves, chopped

¼ cup chopped fresh parsley

¾ pound spaghetti

1. Combine all the meatball ingredients, except the olive oil, in a large bowl. Blend thoroughly with your hands until completely mixed together. Form into 12 meatballs of equal size.

2. Heat the olive oil in a large skillet over medium heat. Add the meatballs and cover. Turn the meatballs every few minutes to brown on all sides until cooked through, about 15 minutes. Remove to a plate.

3. Heat the olive oil for the sauce in a large pot over medium heat. Add the onions, season with salt and pepper, and cook until the onions are translucent and soft.

4. Add the tomato paste, garlic, and red pepper flakes and cook for another 2 to 3 minutes, or until the paste starts to caramelize.

5. Add the crushed tomatoes, sugar, and oregano to the pot, along with 1 cup water. Season with salt and pepper to taste. Stir and bring to a simmer over medium-low heat.

6. Add the meatballs to the pot and let simmer for 20 minutes. Add the basil and parsley and let simmer for an additional 5 minutes.

7. While the sauce is simmering, bring a large pot of salted water to a boil. Add the spaghetti and cook for about 8 to 10 minutes, or until al dente. Drain the pasta and add it back into the pot. Add a few ladles of sauce and mix.

8. Transfer the pasta to a large serving bowl and top with just enough sauce to coat the noodles. Transfer the remaining sauce and meatballs to a large bowl and serve alongside the spaghetti.

MEAT

I CAN'T TALK ABOUT MEAT WITHOUT THINKING ABOUT VIENNA, AUSTRIA. I was there the first time for an international skating competition when I was fourteen. It was only my second time going abroad, so I was pretty awestruck by the city. Vienna is truly "old-world" in the finest European tradition. I was impressed by the amazing mix of apartment buildings that were centuries old, standing right next to modern architecture. A lot of the streets were cobblestone, and there were statues and public gardens everywhere you looked.

But the best part of the whole trip for me (besides winning the competition) was tasting entrecôte for the first time. Entrecôte is the French name for a cut of beef taken from between the ribs, and it is amazingly tender and tasty. I ordered it the first night in a restaurant around the corner from the hotel, and wound up going back there almost every night.

The steak was cooked perfectly, much rarer than my mom would ever have cooked meat. It was served with béarnaise, a simple, rich sauce that is dominated by the subtle licorice flavor of tarragon. It was the first time I became aware of how much a single herb can impact a whole dish. These types of mouthwatering flavor combinations are what I try to keep in mind whenever I'm preparing meat, as I did in the Grilled Flank Steak with Arugula Gremolata (opposite).

RIB-STICKING BEEF

When I was a kid, we didn't have the Food Network or the Cooking Channel, and there weren't any foodies. Dinners in my house were on a seven-day schedule. Monday was fish, Tuesday was pork chop day, and Wednesday was "wildcard day" when Mom would make whatever was convenient. My favorite day, though, was by far Sunday. Sunday was beef day. Actually, it was chateaubriand day.

My mom had a few special dishes, and chateaubriand was one of her best. She made a sauce with shallots and tarragon and red wine vinegar. That simple sauce complemented the meat without overwhelming it, or being too light to have an impact. That kind of balance was the inspiration for the Pan-Roasted Filet Mignon with Balsamic Syrup and Asparagus on page 113.

Of course, each type of beef has its own nuances when it comes to flavor, and there are different ways to bring out those nuances. Personally, I absolutely love braising beef so that it's fall-off-the-bone tender, like the Short Rib Bourguignon on page 118. No matter what cut of beef you prefer, you'll find lots of flavor combinations in the recipes that follow.

GRILLED FLANK STEAK *with* ARUGULA GREMOLATA

Flank steak is easy to cook, especially when you use this flavor-rich gremolata to tenderize the steak. A gremolata has a super-fresh flavor and is made with just a few basic ingredients. A traditional gremolata is an Italian condiment—basically chopped parsley, garlic, and lemon zest. But there are a lot of variations out there. Mine incorporates arugula for a little spicy flavor. You can switch it up by adding your own favorite herbs or other ingredients like kalamata olives. This sauce is so versatile that I usually make more than I need, and keep it on hand to use on everything from other meats and chicken to sandwiches! As far as the meat goes, if you can't find flank steak, top round or flatiron cuts will do just as well in a pinch.

SERVES 4

6 cloves garlic

1 cup Italian flat-leaf parsley

2 cups arugula

Zest of 1 lemon

Zest of 1 orange

1 tablespoon red wine vinegar

½ cup olive oil, plus 1 tablespoon

Salt and freshly ground black pepper to taste

1½ pounds flank steak

BRIAN'S KITCHEN POINTER

Lettuces don't often come in small, precise amounts, so you'll probably have some arugula left over from this recipe. Consider using it in the Arugula and Nectarine Salad with Pepperoncini Vinaigrette and Olive Bread Croutons on page 71, or in the Grilled Steak Sandwich with Goat Cheese, Dijon, and Roasted Peppers on page 43.

1. Add the garlic to a food processor fitted with the blade attachment and pulse to chop. Add the parsley, arugula, citrus zests, vinegar, 1 tablespoon olive oil, and salt and pepper to taste. Pulse until the mixture is finely chopped.

2. Remove half of the gremolata from the processor to a container. Cover and refrigerate until you're ready to use.

3. Add the remaining olive oil to the remaining gremolata and pulse to blend.

4. Place the steak in a large resealable bag and pour the gremolata-and-olive-oil mixture over the steak. Toss the steak to coat. Let it sit out for 30 minutes.

5. Preheat the grill to medium-high heat.

6. Remove the steak from the marinade and shake off any excess. Season with salt and pepper and grill for 3 to 4 minutes per side. Let the steak rest for 5 minutes before slicing it against the grain into ½-thick strips.

7. Arrange the steak on a serving platter and top with the reserved gremolata.

CARNE ASADA TACOS *with* GREEN SALSA

I made these tacos on my TV show for Kristi Yamaguchi, when she brought her family to dinner. I love spending time with the Yamaguchis, and when they came over, I didn't want to spend half the night in the kitchen. That's what makes this recipe so great for entertaining. With the exception of prepping for the braising, there is very little work to do. And there is no time crunch because you can keep the meat warm in the liquid until you're ready to serve without concern of overcooking it. You prepare everything beforehand and let the meat cook "low and slow" (a long time at a low temperature). The beef can even be braised the day before; just be sure to reheat it in the braising liquid to keep it moist.

SERVES 6–8

CARNE ASADA:

2 cups vegetable stock or broth

1 (28-ounce) can diced tomatoes

2 chipotle peppers

1 medium yellow onion, chopped

4 cloves garlic, chopped

2 tablespoons ground cumin

2 tablespoons chili powder

2 teaspoons salt

2 teaspoons freshly ground black
   pepper

4 pounds beef round roast

CARNE ASADA:

1. Preheat the oven to 325°F.

2. To make the carne asada, add the stock, tomatoes, chipotle peppers, onions, and garlic to a Dutch oven and stir to combine.

3. Combine the cumin, chili powder, salt, and black pepper in a small bowl. Sprinkle the spice mixture over the beef so that it is evenly coated.

4. Put the seasoned beef into the Dutch oven and cover. Braise in the oven until the meat is fork tender, about 3 hours.

5. Remove the beef from the pot and put it into a baking dish. Shred with 2 forks and drizzle with some of the braising liquid to keep the meat moist. Cover with aluminum foil until ready to serve.

BRIAN'S KITCHEN POINTER

One of the great things about chipotle peppers (and there are so many great things) is that you can use fresh or canned for this recipe. If you go with canned, place the leftover peppers in a resealable container and keep them in the refrigerator for later uses. You can always add the remaining peppers to sour cream or mayo as a spread for sandwiches, or use them in your favorite vinaigrette. You can even add them to the black bean salsa that goes into the Southwestern Sopapillas on page 10, the Sweet Corn Chowder on page 58, or the Grilled Corn, Jicama, and Bean Salad on page 66.

GREEN SALSA:

2 poblano peppers

4 tomatillos, peeled of outer skin and chopped

2 avocados, halved, pitted, peeled, and flesh diced

2 cloves garlic, chopped

Juice of 1 lime

¼ bunch fresh cilantro, chopped

1 tablespoon white vinegar

Pinch of salt and freshly ground black pepper, plus more for seasoning

TACOS:

3 cups canola oil

24 corn tortillas

24 small flour tortillas

1 small head green cabbage, shredded

2 cups crumbled *queso fresco*

GREEN SALSA:

1. To make the salsa, first preheat the broiler. Place the poblano peppers on a sheet pan under the broiler for 8 minutes, turning every 2 minutes until the skins are charred.

2. Remove the pan from the broiler, transfer the peppers to a bowl, cover with plastic wrap, and let sit to allow the skin to separate from the flesh, about 10 minutes.

3. Core, seed, and peel the charred skin from the peppers.

4. Combine the peppers with the remaining salsa ingredients in a blender, holding three-quarters of the diced avocado in reserve. Puree the mixture until smooth.

5. Pour the salsa into a medium bowl and add the remaining diced avocado. Gently toss the salsa with a rubber spatula to coat the avocado. Taste and adjust the seasonings with more salt and pepper, if desired. Set aside.

TACOS:

1. To make the tacos, heat the canola oil in a large skillet over medium heat until it reaches 350°F.

2. Fry the corn tortillas in batches until crispy but still slightly pliable, about 2 to 3 minutes. Transfer them to a sheet tray lined with paper towels to drain any excess oil.

3. Place the flour tortillas in a damp towel and microwave for 45 seconds on high to soften them.

4. Arrange a fried corn tortilla on each flour tortilla. Spoon some of the beef onto the corn tortilla. Top with shredded cabbage, 2 tablespoons green salsa, and 1 tablespoon *queso fresco*.

5. Repeat with the remaining ingredients. Arrange on a serving platter and serve.

PAN-ROASTED FILET MIGNON *with* BALSAMIC SYRUP *and* ASPARAGUS

At 5 feet, 6 inches and 125 pounds, my dad can really put away the food. He will sometimes finish his meal and what's left over from mom's meal. He loves an incredibly tender filet mignon, but he's not much of a sauce man. However, the one sauce he really likes is this balsamic syrup reduction. It's sweet and tangy. Try it as a dip for crusty artisanal bread or as a coating on tuna steak—it's even terrific drizzled over strawberries for dessert. It's amazing the many things you can use this sauce on. The balsamic syrup can also be made in advance, and will last up to two weeks in a sealed container stored in the refrigerator. Reheat just before using. If you're not a fan of asparagus, try substituting green beans.

SERVES 4

1½ pounds asparagus

1¼ pounds filet mignon, cut into 4
    equal portions

Salt and freshly ground black pepper
    to taste

3 tablespoons canola oil

6 tablespoons butter

3 cloves garlic, smashed

5 sprigs fresh thyme

2 tablespoons olive oil

1 cup balsamic vinegar

1 tablespoon brown sugar

1. Slice 1½ inches off the bottom of the asparagus, while bringing a large pot of water to a boil over high heat.

2. Add the asparagus to the pot and blanch for 1 minute. Remove the asparagus from the water and shock in an ice bath. Transfer the asparagus from the ice bath to a sheet pan lined with a paper towel.

3. Take the filets out of the refrigerator 20 minutes before cooking, so they can come to room temperature. Season each filet liberally with salt and pepper. Preheat the oven to 300°F.

4. Heat the canola oil in a large heavy-bottomed skillet over high heat. Sear the filets in the skillet until brown and crispy, about 2 minutes per side.

5. Turn the heat to low and add 4 tablespoons of the butter, the garlic, and the fresh thyme. Baste the filets with the melted butter, using a spoon.

6. Place the skillet in the oven for 4 to 5 minutes for medium-rare or until the internal temperature reaches 130°F to 135°F on an instant-read thermometer. Let the filets rest 5 minutes before serving.

7. Heat the olive oil in a large skillet over medium heat. Add the asparagus, season with salt and pepper to taste, and sauté until heated through, about 2 minutes. The asparagus should be slightly tender but still have a little snap when you bite into them.

8. Combine the balsamic vinegar and brown sugar in a small pot over medium-low heat. Whisk to mix. Reduce until thick, about the consistency of maple syrup. Whisk in 2 table-spoons of butter and season with salt and pepper to taste.

9. To serve, lay a bed of 6 asparagus on a plate. Arrange a filet mignon on top and drizzle with the balsamic reduction. Repeat with all the filets. Serve immediately.

WEST COAST BURGERS

When I was a kid, the first thing we'd all do when we went to visit my Aunt Tree's beach house was head down to a burger joint called Sno White Burgers. They were—and are—char-grilled fresh, and come with a special sauce that is basically Thousand Island dressing. This West Coast burger is my tip of the hat to those incredible hamburgers. I use a three-meat blend with just enough fat content to keep the burgers dense and juicy. And it comes with my own version of special sauce. Have your butcher grind the meat to order, using a coarse grind. The coarse grind creates a looser burger, which will keep it tender.

SERVES 6

GRILLED ONIONS:

2 tablespoons canola oil

2 medium yellow onions, diced

2 tablespoons yellow mustard

Pinch of salt

SPECIAL SAUCE:

⅓ cup mayonnaise

3 tablespoons ketchup

1 tablespoon yellow mustard

1 tablespoon hot sauce

½ teaspoon garlic powder

½ teaspoon paprika

BURGERS:

1 pound ground meat (equal parts
   sirloin, chuck, and brisket)

2 tablespoons canola oil

2 teaspoons salt

2 teaspoons freshly ground black
   pepper

1 teaspoon garlic powder

6 slices American cheese

6 soft potato hamburger rolls
   (recommended: Martin's brand)

3 tablespoons butter, melted

2 plum tomatoes, cut into ¼-inch-thick
   slices

6 green-leaf lettuce leaves

1. Heat the canola oil in a large skillet over medium heat. Add the onions and cook until soft and lightly caramelized, about 15 minutes.

2. Add the mustard and a pinch of salt and cook for another 2 minutes. Remove the onions from the pan to a small bowl and set aside.

3. Combine all the ingredients for the special sauce in a medium bowl. Whisk until smooth.

4. Preheat the broiler.

5. Form the ground meat mixture into 6 equal patties. Do not overhandle or compress the patties; keep them loose. (This will help create a tender burger. Overmixing and compacting will result in a tough burger.)

6. Heat the canola oil in a large heavy-bottomed skillet over medium-high heat.

7. Combine the salt, pepper, and garlic powder in a small bowl. Season the burgers generously with the mixture.

8. Place the patties in the skillet and cook for 4 minutes. Flip and let cook for 1 minute more, then top each patty with a piece of cheese. Cook for another 2 minutes, until the cheese is melted and the burgers are medium.

9. While the burgers are cooking, lightly brush the buns with melted butter and put them on a sheet pan. Broil until lightly toasted.

10. To assemble, spread each bun half with about a tablespoon of the special sauce. Put a burger on the bottom half of each bun and top with caramelized onions, tomato, and lettuce. Cover with the top half of the bun and serve.

BRIAN'S KITCHEN POINTER

Turn these burgers into a great party snack by making them into "sliders." Make the burgers bite-size and put them on tiny rolls, just like the ones used with the Paella Sliders (page 4). Make it fun and give your guests more options by topping a few with cheese, a couple with olive tapenade, and maybe even some with sautéed mushrooms. Just remember to save some sliders for the guests.

SHORT RIB BOURGUIGNON

My niece Krista, who lives in Iowa, is a college student and recently discovered cooking. I am pleased to say she calls Uncle Brian with questions about chopping, seasoning, and baking, and sometimes just to talk about her burgeoning interest. She is beginning to understand the alchemy of cooking, which is gratifying. When she saw the movie *Julie & Julia,* she wanted to make Julia Child's Boeuf Bourguignon. After slaving away, she called me with this observation: "Uncle Brian, I think you can do better." Who am I to disappoint my niece? So I accepted the challenge and came up with this dish. And even though I wouldn't compare it to Julia's, Krista thinks it's absolutely delicious.

I begin with short ribs, which are on my list of best-ever foods, and cook them until the meat falls from the bones. The rich-tasting braising liquid has multiple uses. It can be served with the Roasted Winter Vegetables on page 182, or spooned over thick egg noodles and topped with shaved Parmesan.

SERVES 4

8 beef short ribs (about 4 pounds), each 3 to 4 inches long

Salt and freshly ground black pepper to taste

2 tablespoons olive oil

4 slices bacon

2 carrots, chopped coarsely

2 stalks celery, chopped coarsely

1 medium yellow onion, chopped coarsely

4 ounces baby portobello (cremini) mushrooms (6 to 8 mushrooms), stemmed and halved

3 tablespoons tomato paste

3 cloves garlic, chopped

1½ cups dry red wine

1 (28-ounce) can diced tomatoes

1 cup beef stock

2 bay leaves

8 sprigs fresh thyme

2 tablespoons red wine vinegar

1. Season the short ribs generously with the salt and pepper.

2. Heat the olive oil in a large Dutch oven or similar pot over medium-high heat. When hot, sear the short ribs for about 5 minutes on each side. Transfer to a plate.

3. Pour out all but 2 tablespoons of the rendered fat from the Dutch oven. Reduce the heat to medium and cook the bacon for about 8 minutes, or until brown and crispy.

4. Cool the bacon on a plate lined with paper towels. When cool enough to handle, break into 1-inch pieces. Set aside.

5. Blend the carrots, celery, onion, and mushrooms in a food processor fitted with a metal blade, until finely ground but not pureed.

6. Add the vegetables to the Dutch oven, season with salt and pepper to taste, and cook over medium heat for 12 to 15 minutes, or until most of the liquid from the vegetables has evaporated and they are slightly caramelized.

7. Add the tomato paste and garlic to the Dutch oven and cook for 3 to 4 minutes. Add the wine and cook for 3 minutes more. Add the diced tomatoes with their juices, the beef stock, bay leaves, thyme, and vinegar. Stir to mix well.

8. Add the seared short ribs to the Dutch oven. Make sure to nestle them into the other ingredients so that they are completely covered with the liquid.

9. Cover the pot, reduce the heat to low, and cook for 2½ to 3 hours, or until the meat is very tender and falls off the bone with little help. Transfer to a serving bowl and serve, sprinkled with the bacon.

BEEF STIR-FRY *with* CABBAGE, PEPPERS, *and* ONIONS

My friend Franc ate exclusively Italian food for most of his life. When he moved to San Francisco, he visited Chinatown and became enthralled by all the different foods he saw there—so enthralled, in fact, that he bought a wok and needed me to show him how to use it. I took him shopping so we could make beef stir-fry. There's nothing like cooking with a wok when you want to whip up some super-delicious stir-fry, and have a ton of fun doing it.

You can easily turn this into a vegetarian dish by substituting tofu for the beef and adding a pound of chopped blanched asparagus. Because the wok cooks food so quickly, you can prepare everything before your friends arrive, and then cook the entire meal in minutes before you finish your first cocktail of the evening! By the way, Franc has since been given the nickname Stir-Fry Master.

SERVES 4

½ cup low-sodium soy sauce

3 tablespoons rice wine vinegar

1 tablespoon hot sauce (recommended: Sriracha)

1 pound flank steak

3 tablespoons canola oil

1 medium yellow onion, sliced

1 small yellow bell pepper, sliced

1 small red bell pepper, cored, seeded, and julienned

½ small head green cabbage, shredded

2 cloves garlic chopped

1 tablespoon chopped fresh ginger

2 teaspoons cornstarch

1 tablespoon brown sugar

1. In a large bowl, whisk together the soy sauce, vinegar, and hot sauce.

2. Slice the flank steak against the grain into thin pieces. Add to the bowl, toss to coat, and let sit for 10 minutes.

3. Heat the canola oil in a large wok over high heat.

4. Remove the steak from the soy sauce mixture and pat dry on a paper towel. Reserve soy sauce mixture. When the oil starts to smoke, add the steak and cook for 3 minutes, stirring often. Remove to a plate.

5. Add the onion and bell peppers to the wok and cook for 2 minutes, stirring often. Add the cabbage, garlic, and ginger and cook for another 2 minutes, stirring continuously.

6. Whisk the cornstarch and brown sugar into the soy sauce mixture. Add to the wok and cook until the liquid comes to a simmer and thickens, or about 1 to 2 minutes.

7. Add the steak to the wok and stir. Transfer to a serving platter.

BRIAN'S KITCHEN POINTER

The ingredients in this recipe can leave you with some leftovers that often get thrown out. If you have leftover ginger and don't plan on using it for awhile, chop it up, place it in a resealable bag, and freeze it. Ginger will keep for up to two months in the freezer. The remaining half head of cabbage can be used to make coleslaw or as a topping for tacos. To store it, wrap the cut side in a damp paper towel, wrap with plastic wrap, and place in the vegetable drawer in the refrigerator.

PITCH-PERFECT PORK

One of the great things about traveling as much as I do is discovering new dishes in faraway places. Maybe the most surprising dish (in a good way) I ever came across was the pork knuckle I had in Germany. I was skating in Olympic gold medalist Katarina Witt's farewell tour in 2008. The tour took us all throughout her native country. When you're on tour you usually don't have a chance to make your own meals, so we ate out almost every night. We sampled all kinds of places, from traditional biergartens (if you love beer, Germany's the place for you!), to small inns, to high-end restaurants. No matter where we went, though, the same dishes popped up fairly regularly on the menus. One of these was pork knuckle, or what the Germans call *schweinshaxe* (we call it ham hock in the United States). It is everywhere you go in Germany. This cut is the upper portion of the leg, so it's not ham and not foot. And, man, is it a lot of pork.

Katarina explained to me that, among Germans, pork knuckle is considered "tourist food." Not only is the meat thick with salty flavor, but it can be pulled apart with a fork. I was surprised to find out that she had never tried it. I convinced her to take a bite, and she liked it. I think I need to e-mail her and see if she has ordered it again since. Next time I go to her house for a visit, I have a pork dish I think she will really like—the Braised Hawaiian Pork Shoulder on page 124.

GRILLED SAUSAGE *and* SWEET GYPSY PEPPERS *with* MUSTARD SAUCE

This recipe was from a refrigerator roundup night. That's when you use ingredients you already have in your refrigerator to make dinner. That night I had a couple different kinds of sausage on hand, and I had some gypsy peppers from another meal I had made two nights before. Gypsy peppers are a sweet pepper varietal, and if your store doesn't carry them, you can use red or yellow bell peppers. This sauce puts the "must" in mustard, because we all know mustard and sausage go so well together.

SERVES 4

8 spicy Italian pork sausage links

3 tablespoons olive oil

3 gypsy peppers, cleaned and sliced

2 medium yellow onions, sliced

Salt and freshly ground black pepper

2 cloves garlic, chopped

½ cup cooking sherry

½ cup chicken broth

¼ cup Dijon mustard

1. Preheat the grill on medium heat. Grill the sausage for about 16 minutes, turning a quarter turn every 4 minutes.

2. While the sausage is cooking, heat the olive oil in a large skillet over medium heat. Add the peppers and onions and season with salt and pepper. Cook for 8 to 10 minutes, stirring every few minutes, until slightly tender.

3. Add the garlic and cook for 2 minutes. Remove sausage, peppers, onions, and garlic to a platter.

4. Add the sherry and chicken broth to the skillet and whisk in the mustard. Reduce the heat to medium-low and cook for about 5 minutes, or until reduced by a third and thickened.

5. Place the sausage on the platter on top of the peppers and onions. Pour the sauce over the top and serve.

BRIAN'S KITCHEN POINTER

I already got started on mustard in the recipe, so let's discuss. There are so many different types, all with their own characteristics, textures, and flavors, that you're really missing out if you don't have a collection of different mustards in your kitchen. Start with a grainy country mustard, a sharp Dijon, and a plain yellow mustard. Then move on to flavored and spicy versions, like tarragon or spicy brown. They come in handy for preparing sauces and dressings, and go with so many different meats and other foods that you'll be glad you stocked up.

BRAISED HAWAIIAN PORK SHOULDER

You will get rave reviews when you serve this. It's amazingly tender, and the blend of spices gives it a flavor that's out of this world. There are deep earthy flavors from the paprika and cumin, and the coriander adds a little fruity tone that really brightens up the rich, savory flavor of the pork. The secret ingredient, though, is the pineapple juice. It not only adds a fruity sweetness to the dish, but the enzymes in the juice naturally tenderize the pork—meaning no knife required when you go to eat it. Another thing I like is how good the kitchen smells for hours. I always try to make extra so that I can have some for sandwiches the next day, but it usually disappears as soon as it hits the table.

SERVES 4

1 tablespoon brown sugar

2 teaspoons red Hawaiian sea salt or kosher salt

2 teaspoons paprika

½ teaspoon ground cumin

½ teaspoon ground coriander

½ teaspoon freshly ground black pepper

1½ pounds pork shoulder (Boston butt)

¼ cup canola oil, divided

1 yellow onion, chopped

1 (3-inch) piece ginger, sliced

4 cloves garlic, peeled and smashed

1 cup pineapple juice

2 cups chicken stock

1. Combine the brown sugar, salt, paprika, cumin, coriander, and black pepper in a small bowl.

2. Cut the pork into 4 equal portions, then tie each cut with butcher's twine. Lightly sprinkle each piece with 1½ teaspoons of the spice mixture.

3. Preheat the oven to 300°F.

4. Heat 3 tablespoons of canola oil in a large Dutch oven over medium heat. Sear each cut of pork on all sides, then transfer them to a plate.

5. Add the remaining 1 tablespoon of canola oil to the same pot, along with the onions, ginger, and garlic. Sauté for 2 minutes.

6. Pour in the pineapple juice and chicken stock and return the pork to the pot. Cover the pot and put it in the oven to braise until the pork is fork tender, about 2½ hours.

7. Remove the pork from the Dutch oven and arrange the pieces on a baking sheet. Sprinkle each piece with the remaining ½ teaspoon of the spice mixture and put them under the broiler. Broil until their tops are brown and crisp but not burned, about 2 minutes.

8. Transfer the pork to a serving platter and serve with a drizzle of braising liquid.

PORK TENDERLOIN *with* WARM PLUM SALSA

Pork tenderloin is an elegant, simple, and satisfying meal, but the plum salsa really puts this dish over the top. Plums lend themselves for use in a salsa because they don't break down when you cook them. They add a fresh, bright element to the pork by balancing that savory flavor with a little sweet fruit. After it's prepared, this salsa looks absolutely beautiful, and the flavor and color adds tremendously to the appeal of the tender pork. This is a great dish for entertaining because it's low in calories, low in fat, and high in protein without sacrificing flavor. And it is so easy to prepare because the pork is roasted whole and then individually sliced for your guests.

SERVES 4

PORK:

1 pork tenderloin (1 to 1½ pounds)

1 teaspoon salt

1 teaspoon freshly ground black pepper

3 tablespoons olive oil

3 scallions, sliced, for garnish

PLUM SALSA:

2 tablespoons olive oil

1 medium yellow onion, diced

1 teaspoon fresh ginger, minced

2 cloves garlic, chopped

1 small red jalapeño pepper, seeded and finely diced

3 plums, pitted and diced

2 tablespoons apple cider vinegar

Salt and freshly ground black pepper to taste

1. Remove the pork from the refrigerator about 30 minutes before you are ready to cook it and let it come to room temperature. Season all sides of the pork thoroughly with salt and pepper.

2. Preheat the oven to 325°F.

3. Heat the olive oil in a large skillet over medium-high heat. Sear the tenderloin on all sides, about 2 to 3 minutes per side.

4. Place the tenderloin in a baking dish and roast in the oven for 20 to 25 minutes, or until the internal temperature reaches 140°F.

5. While the tenderloin is cooking, make the plum salsa. Heat the olive oil in a large skillet over medium heat. Add the onion, ginger, and garlic and cook for 2 minutes.

6. Add the jalapeño, plums, and vinegar and season with salt and pepper. Cook for 1 to 2 minutes, until just heated through.

7. Let the tenderloin rest for 5 minutes before slicing. Arrange the slices on a serving platter and top with warm plum salsa. Garnish with the scallions.

A LITTLE LAMB

Lamb wasn't something that ever came out of my mom's oven. Back when I was kid, the only lamb I ever saw was served in restaurants. In fact, that's my first memory of lamb—the rack of lamb my mom would order when we went out for dinner. Back in the day, it was quite the presentation. The lamb would come out with all the trimmings, little white caps covering the ends of the bones, and a big ramekin of mint jelly perched on the plate. I think my mom really enjoyed lamb as something different, something she would never make for herself.

Nowadays, there's just no reason not to treat yourself to lamb. It's great grilled, braised, or roasted. As you might imagine, though, I wanted to bring my own, more contemporary twist to cooking lamb.

I'm not a fan of jelly, let alone mint jelly, which is why I added my own spin to the Grilled Rack of Lamb with Red Chimichurri Sauce (below). The distinctive flavoring of the meat is complemented by a vibrant, classic South American red sauce that brings tons of life to a classic dish. Mostly, though, I still think of lamb as an incredible special-occasion meal, and I love to serve it for the holidays.

GRILLED RACK *of* LAMB *with* RED CHIMICHURRI SAUCE

When I was in Argentina, I discovered that chimichurri is like pesto in Genoa, an everyday standard that people use on meat, fish, and poultry. Classic chimichurri is made tart. I wanted to add a little sweetness to balance out the tartness of the vinegar, so I included sun-dried tomatoes and roasted red peppers. (They're so much better than mint jelly!) Rack of lamb looks beautiful on the plate, and even more so with this stunning red sauce.

To make an attractive presentation, the lamb should be "frenched." The meat at the tips and in between the bones is cut away to expose the bones. Although it's not absolutely necessary to do this, it makes for a much nicer appearance. At the very least, make sure your butcher cuts the chine bone, the backbone between the ribs, so that the rack is easy to carve. And by the way, you can forego the paper frills (the little white hats on the end of the bone) too!

SERVES 4

1 rack of lamb (2–2 ½ pounds),
     frenched

1 teaspoon salt

1 teaspoon freshly ground black
     pepper

1 large red bell pepper (the equivalent
     of roasted red peppers from a jar
     can be substituted)

3 cloves garlic, chopped

1 shallot, chopped

1 cup fresh Italian flat-leaf parsley

Juice of 1 lemon

6 sun-dried tomatoes, chopped

¼ cup red wine vinegar

¼ teaspoon red pepper flakes

1 tablespoon paprika

⅓ cup olive oil

Salt and pepper to taste

BRIAN'S KITCHEN POINTER

You may not want to fire up
the grill, but that's OK—you
can cook this lamb in your
oven! Heat a large cast-iron
skillet over medium-high heat.
Place the lamb in the skillet,
fat-side down first, and sear
until it is browned, about 3
to 4 minutes per side. Then
place the skillet in the oven
and roast the lamb at 325°F
for about 15 to 20 minutes, or
until the internal temperature
reaches 130°F for medium-
rare. Remove the lamb from
the oven, cover it with foil, and
let it rest for about 5 minutes
before slicing and serving.

1. Remove the lamb from the refrigerator about
30 minutes before you are ready to cook it and let it
come to room temperature. Season all sides thoroughly
with salt and pepper.

2. Preheat the grill on medium-high heat.

3. Place the lamb on the grill, fat-side down first, and sear
until it is browned, about 3 to 4 minutes per side. Reduce
the heat to low, close the lid, and cook for about 15 to 20
minutes, or until the internal temperature reaches 130°F
for medium-rare. Let the lamb rest for about 10 minutes
before slicing.

4. While the lamb is cooking, preheat the broiler, with the
rack set about 6 inches under the broiler. Place the bell
pepper on a baking sheet and roast it under the broiler for
about 8 to 10 minutes, turning a quarter turn every couple
of minutes until the pepper is charred on all sides.

5. Remove the pepper from the oven, place it in a bowl,
and cover the bowl with plastic wrap. Let the pepper
steam for 10 minutes.

6. Remove the pepper from the bowl and peel off the
skin. (You can use a paper towel to wipe off any small
bits of skin from the pepper.) Carefully core and seed the
pepper, and reserve any liquid that has drained from it.
Slice it into strips and set aside.

7. Combine the pepper with the rest of the ingredients,
including reserved pepper liquid, in a food processor
or blender. Pulse until blended. (The mixture should be
pureed but slightly chunky rather than entirely smooth.)
Taste and add salt and pepper as desired.

8. Serve the rack of lamb with the sauce poured over
the top.

ROSEMARY BRAISED LAMB SHANKS

Once you braise these lamb shanks, you can just about shake the meat off the bone. The rosemary in this recipe accents the super-tender meat. Rosemary is a wonderful herb that's easy to grow year-round and a perfect complement to any meat or poultry. I even like to mix it with butter and a little salt and smear it on a loaf of sliced artisanal bread, then wrap the bread in foil and heat it in the oven for a quick last-minute side to a meal. Other side dishes you may want to try with this recipe are mashed potatoes or polenta. Either one is a great accompaniment to the lamb shanks.

SERVES 4

6 tablespoons olive oil

4 lamb shanks

1 teaspoon salt

1 teaspoon freshly ground black pepper

3 parsnips, peeled and diced coarsely

1 large yellow onion, diced coarsely

1 large bulb fennel, diced coarsely

Salt and pepper to taste

4 cloves garlic, chopped

½ (6-ounce) can tomato paste

2 cups red table wine

1 (15-ounce) can diced tomatoes

4 cups vegetable broth

4 rosemary sprigs, tied together

2 bay leaves

3 tablespoons chopped fresh Italian flat-leaf parsley, for garnish

BRIAN'S KITCHEN POINTER

The remaining vegetables can be served alongside the lamb shanks or you can use them in a soup. Combine them with 4 cups of vegetable stock, heat and serve.

1. Heat 3 tablespoons of olive oil in a large Dutch oven over medium-high heat. Generously season all sides of the shanks with salt and pepper. Sear the shanks, 2 at a time, on all sides until browned. Remove to a plate and set aside.

2. Lower the heat to medium, add the remaining olive oil.

3. Add the parsnips, onions, and fennel. Season with salt and pepper and cook for about 12 to 15 minutes, or until the vegetables begin to caramelize.

4. Preheat the oven to 350°F.

5. Add the garlic and tomato paste and cook for about 3 to 4 minutes, or until the tomato paste begins to caramelize.

6. Add the wine, stir, and let cook for another 3 minutes. Add the tomatoes, vegetable broth, rosemary sprigs, and bay leaves and stir.

7. Nestle the shanks into the liquid so that they are submerged. Cover and place in the oven for 2½ to 3 hours, or until the meat is tender and easily pulls off the bone.

8. Remove the shanks to a platter and cover with foil.

9. Remove the rosemary and bay leaves from the braising liquid. Transfer half the cooked vegetables and three-quarters of the liquid from the pot to a blender making sure to not fill more than two-thirds of the way to the top.

10. Cover with top but vent slightly, cover with a dishtowel, and puree until smooth. It should be about the consistency of thick gravy. If it's too thick, add a bit more of the liquid and blend.

11. Pour the puree over the shanks. Garnish with the chopped parsley and serve immediately.

POULTRY

I REMEMBER MY FIRST TRIP TO THE FAR EAST. A skating tour took me through Korea, Japan, and China, and it was easily the most exotic and eye-opening leg of my travels.

Korea and Japan had their charms, but China was the most interesting country I visited because, although it wasn't exactly closed to outsiders, it wasn't totally open either. Every time I left my hotel, I had a government "escort" as a shadow. The rules were that foreigners could only shop at what they called "Friendship Stores," but when I had a chance to cruise around a real Chinese outdoor market, I jumped at it. There were about a bazillion people there, all on bicycles—it was the most crowded market I've ever seen. And it was the first time in my life I had ever seen live chickens for sale, and freshly slaughtered birds hanging by their necks.

There was a food cart nearby that was selling chicken dishes and, being young and brave (or maybe naive), I decided to try some of the very local cuisine. I was a little skeptical about a food cart in downtown Beijing, but I got lucky—it was really wonderful stir-fried chicken with garlic sauce.

That wasn't the end of my adventures, though. Any visit to China is hardly complete unless you sample Peking Duck. I tasted that national delicacy for the first time in Hong Kong, during a big ice-skating banquet. Authentic Peking Duck is an incredibly rich dish, with juicy, fatty meat and crispy skin, making for an incredible mixture of flavors and textures . . . all wrapped up in doughy miniature pancakes.

That trip taught me a lot about food in the Far East, including the many ways poultry can be prepared differently than in other parts of the world. Chicken is like the blank canvas for cooking. The use of spices and sauces can be used to make chicken a really interesting dish, like the salty spiciness and light sweetness in the Thai Red Curry Chicken on page 138.

CHICKEN *and* TOMATO STEW *with* TOASTED POLENTA

Made with beef, this recipe would be something like a peasant's stew, perfect for cold weather. Made with chicken, the dish is a little lighter and works in any season. It's still hearty and filling, and the toasted polenta is a crunchy addition to the meal. Add your favorite beans if you have your heart set on a more filling, stew-like meal, or eat this dish as is, for some simple, Mediterranean-style goodness.

This stew can be made up to two days ahead of time and reheated on the stove over medium-low heat. To save time, you can use quick-cook polenta. If there is any leftover stew sauce, you can make another meal by serving it over pasta.

SERVES 4

STEW:

⅓ cup all-purpose flour

1 teaspoon salt

1 teaspoon freshly ground black pepper

1 whole chicken (about 5 pounds), cut up into pieces

5 tablespoons olive oil

1 large yellow onion, sliced

4 cloves garlic, chopped

3 tablespoons tomato paste

1½ cups dry red wine

1 cup chicken stock

1 (28-ounce) can whole plum tomatoes, crushed by hand

1 teaspoon dried oregano

10 basil leaves, torn; reserve a bit for garnish

3 tablespoons chopped Italian flat-leaf parsley; reserve a bit for garnish

STEW:

1. Combine the flour, salt, and pepper in a small bowl. Dust the chicken pieces with the flour mixture, making sure each piece is coated on all sides.

2. Heat 3 tablespoons of olive oil in a large Dutch oven over medium-high heat. Cook half the chicken pieces for about 3 to 4 minutes per side, or until nicely browned. Remove to a plate covered with a paper towel.

3. Add the remaining olive oil to the Dutch oven and brown the remaining chicken, setting it aside when done.

4. Add the onions to the Dutch oven, reduce the heat to medium, and cook for 3 to 4 minutes or until softened, stirring occasionally. Add the garlic and cook for 1 minute more.

5. Add the tomato paste and cook for another 2 to 3 minutes, stirring constantly, until the paste begins to caramelize.

6. Stir in the wine and cook for 3 minutes. Add the chicken stock, tomatoes, and herbs and bring to a simmer.

7. Return the chicken pieces to the Dutch oven and nestle them into the liquid so that they are covered. Cover, reduce heat to low, and cook for 45 minutes.

POLENTA:

5 cups chicken broth

1½ cups polenta

½ cup light cream

¼ cup grated Parmesan

POLENTA:

1. While the chicken cooks, bring the chicken broth to a boil in a large pot over medium heat. Meanwhile, add the polenta to a skillet over medium heat and toast for 3 to 4 minutes.

2. Slowly add the toasted polenta to the chicken broth in a thin stream, whisking constantly. Reduce the heat to low and cook, stirring often with a wooden spoon, until the polenta is thickened and tender, about 35 minutes.

3. Add the cream and Parmesan and cook for another 5 minutes. The polenta should be thick but pourable. Taste and add salt if desired.

4. Divide the polenta between 4 shallow bowls. Top each with some of the chicken and sauce, garnish with the reserved basil and parsley, and serve.

SPANISH CHICKEN *with* PEPPERS *and* OLIVES

True confession: I am an olive-holic. Black or green, if there are olives in the dish, count me in. The Spanish definitely know how to cook with olives, and I've stolen a page from that country's playbook in marrying olives to a chicken dish with a tempting smokiness. You might want to create an extra-large batch of the annatto oil used in this recipe. The color is such a vibrant red that it actually was used for dying fabrics. I always keep some on hand with my other oils, because it adds an absolutely earthy flavor perfect for cooking all kinds of dishes, from chicken and pork to seafood.

SERVES 4

⅓ cup olive oil

1½ tablespoons annatto seeds

4 boneless, skinless chicken breasts

Salt and freshly ground black pepper to taste

1 large yellow onion, diced

1 red bell pepper, seeded and diced

3 cloves garlic, chopped

1 cup short-grain Spanish rice

2 cups chicken broth

1 teaspoon smoked paprika

¾ cup coarsely chopped pitted green olives

¼ cup chopped Italian flat-leaf parsley

1. Combine the olive oil and annatto seeds in a small pot. Heat over low heat for 4 to 5 minutes, until the temperature reaches 275°F.

2. Remove from the heat and let cool to room temperature. Pour the oil through cheesecloth to strain the seeds out, and discard the seeds.

3. Generously season both sides of the chicken breasts with salt and pepper.

4. Heat half of the annatto oil in a large high-sided skillet over medium-high heat. Brown the chicken on both sides and transfer to a plate covered with paper towels.

5. Add the remaining annatto oil to the skillet, along with the onion, pepper, and garlic. Sauté for 3 minutes.

6. Add the rice and cook for another 2 minutes. Stir in the chicken broth, paprika, olives, and half of the parsley, and season with salt and pepper to taste.

7. Add the cooked chicken, cover, and reduce the heat to low. Cook until all the liquid has been absorbed and the rice is tender, about 15 to 20 minutes.

8. Remove the rice to a serving plate, top with the chicken breasts, and garnish with the remaining parsley.

THAI RED CURRY CHICKEN

I first had curry in Hong Kong, where they rated it from one to four stars, depending on how spicy you wanted it. I was a one-star kind of guy, and this is a one-star dish. But although it's not super hot, it does capture that exotic blend of flavors that make curry such a favorite food worldwide. This recipe also adds a bit of traditional Thai flair with the addition of fish sauce and coconut milk. You can always make this into your own four-star dish by adding more curry paste. (I'm really trying to make my way up to at least three stars.) This recipe also works great with shrimp; just substitute large shelled and deveined shrimp for the chicken.

SERVES 4

4 cups cooked jasmine rice

2 tablespoons canola oil

1 red bell pepper, sliced

1 large yellow onion, sliced

3 cloves garlic, chopped

1 tablespoon chopped fresh ginger

1 tablespoon Thai red curry paste

1 (14-ounce) can coconut milk

¾ cup chicken stock

1 tablespoon brown sugar

2 tablespoons fish sauce

1 pound boneless chicken breast, sliced into thin, bite-size pieces

Juice of 1 lime

¼ cup coarsely chopped fresh Thai basil

¼ cup coarsely chopped fresh cilantro

1. Cook the jasmine rice according to the package directions. While it is cooking, heat the canola oil in large skillet or wok over high heat.

2. Add the sliced peppers and onions to the wok and cook for 2 minutes, stirring occasionally.

3. Add the garlic, ginger, and curry paste and cook for 1 minute, stirring occasionally.

4. Add the coconut milk, chicken stock, brown sugar, and fish sauce and bring to a simmer over medium heat.

5. Stir in the chicken pieces and simmer for 5 to 6 minutes, or until the chicken is cooked through. Stir in the lime juice, basil, and cilantro.

6. Serve the stir-fry mix over the jasmine rice.

SPICE-RUBBED BRICK CORNISH GAME HENS

A couple years ago I purchased a new barbecue, and I had a hard time regulating the temperature. My sister Lynn convinced me (or maybe I convinced her, but this makes a better story) to do beer-can Cornish game hens for Thanksgiving that year. We burned the hens so badly, they were almost pure char. Lynn spent the next hour trying to salvage something edible under the charred skin.

I like using game hens for entertaining because everyone gets their own bird, and usually in just the right proportion. Lesson learned, I switched from beer cans to bricks, figured out how to use my barbecue, and the family is happy. This is a simple and fun cooking method to use with any bird, and it always makes for incredibly tender meat with super-crunchy skin, especially if you use the stovetop-and-oven method. To save time, you can ask your butcher to butterfly the hens for you.

SERVES 4

2 tablespoons paprika

2 teaspoons garlic powder

2 teaspoons onion powder

1 teaspoon chili powder

1 teaspoon ground coriander

¼ teaspoon cayenne pepper

1 tablespoon salt

2 teaspoons freshly ground
    black pepper

1 teaspoon brown sugar

4 Cornish game hens

6 tablespoons canola oil

1. Combine all the spices and sugar in a small bowl and stir together with a fork until completely blended.

2. Place the Cornish game hens on a cutting board. Use a sharp knife or kitchen shears to cut along both sides of the backbone and remove it. Open the bird up so that the drumsticks point out, and press down on the breast to flatten the breastbone.

3. Place the hens on a baking sheet and generously season both sides of each hen with the spice mixture. Rub the mixture into both the skin and the meat. Cover with plastic and place in the refrigerator for at least 2 hours, or as long as overnight.

4. Preheat the grill on medium. Brush the grill grates with oil to prevent sticking.

5. Place the birds, breast-side up, on the grill. Place a sheet pan on top of the hens and weigh down the sheet pan with 2 bricks or with a large cast-iron skillet.

6. Close the grill and cook for 8 to 10 minutes. Remove the sheet pan, flip the hens, replace the pan and bricks, close the grill, and cook for another 8 to 10 minutes. (If the hens begin to char, reduce the heat to medium-low.)

7. Grill until a thermometer stuck in a hen registers 165°F. Remove the hens to a platter and let rest for 5 minutes before serving

OPTIONAL STOVETOP-AND-OVEN METHOD

If you don't have a grill or just don't want to fire it up, use this cooking method instead.

1. Follow steps 1 through 3 opposite.

2. Preheat the oven to 400°F. Wrap 2 bricks completely in foil.

3. Heat 3 tablespoons of canola oil in a large cast-iron skillet over medium-high heat. Place 2 game hens, breast-side down, in the skillet and put a brick on top of each hen. Lower the heat to medium and cook until the skin is browned, about 8 to 10 minutes.

4. Remove the bricks, turn the hens over, replace the bricks, and cook for 8 minutes more. Repeat the process with the remaining 2 hens.

5. Transfer the hens, breast-side up, to a sheet pan fitted with a rack. Place another sheet pan on top of the hens and put the bricks on top of the sheet pan.

6. Cook in the oven for 10 minutes, or until a thermometer stuck in a hen registers 165°F. Remove to a platter and let rest 5 minutes before serving.

SEAFOOD

MY AUNT TREE'S BEACH HOUSE HAS A WRAPAROUND DECK with an incredible view out over the ocean. That view includes a cement ship sunk in the shallows right off the beach. No, I'm not kidding. It's a ship made out of cement.

It was the SS *Palo Alto,* a tanker built at the end of World War I. I guess cement ships didn't really catch on, because this one was mothballed a few years after it was built, and it was later sunk off the Northern California coast to be used as a restaurant and small amusement park. That didn't work out too well either; it cracked in half. After that, it was just used as a fishing pier, and it was one of my favorite places to hang out as a kid.

Whenever we were there, my brother would go fishing and I would watch. He would throw back any fish he caught, but lots of locals lined the sides of the cement ship, fishing for their dinner. Between those fishermen and the crabbers, it was the first time I became aware that you can actually pull your food right out of the ocean.

This chapter is all about the two types of seafood: rich, sweet crustaceans like the classic Shrimp and Polenta on page 152, and healthy, milder fish like Seared Halibut with Grilled Tomato Sauce and Sautéed Artichoke Hearts on page 155.

MARVELISH SHELLFISH

My first memories of San Francisco are of Fisherman's Wharf. You smell salt water, hear seagulls, and, most of all, you see lots and lots of shellfish at outdoor stands.

My mom and dad would take us kids to the city almost every other weekend. There were lots of great places to go, but around lunchtime we'd always wind up back at Fisherman's Wharf. There were piles of fresh-cooked crab legs, tanks of live lobsters, clams and oysters on cracked ice, and fields of shrimp just waiting for some cocktail sauce. I loved it as a little kid, and I still do.

Once we'd all worked up a hearty appetite walking around the docks, we would have lunch at one of the famous old classic restaurants like Alioto's, Scoma's, or my mom and dad's favorite: Pompeii's Grotto. It's a tourist destination for sure, but locals like me keep going back for the charm and incredibly fresh seafood.

There is another classic place on the wharf where I still get my favorite seafood dish every couple of months. In fact, it's named for the dish: Cioppino's (check out my spin on this shellfish classic on page 150). In my opinion, cioppino is a filling, incredibly delicious soup-stew that is light on the stomach. Just the smell of it brings back a flood of great memories and reinforces my connection to, and love for, San Francisco.

CRISPY CRAB CAKES
with AVOCADO-CITRUS SALAD

To me, a great crab cake has a really crunchy exterior and sweet, tender lump crabmeat inside. There are so many options on how to serve them. I sometimes set them on just a bed of simple sautéed greens, but in this dish I use a side salad. The light citrus and tart flavors of the salad go well with the rich flavor of the crab and the spicy aioli tops it off nicely. If you are serving the crab cakes on sautéed greens, or just alone, I like to use the remoulade (page 147). Don't be shy about experimenting with different greens—Swiss chard, for instance, would be great with these crab cakes!

SERVES 4

SPICY AIOLI:

½ cup mayonnaise

¼ cup sour cream

2 teaspoons hot sauce

Juice of 1 lemon

CRAB CAKES:

1 pound lump Dungeness crabmeat

3 cups fresh bread crumbs, toasted (divided)

2 tablespoons mayonnaise

1 tablespoon Dijon mustard

1 teaspoon hot sauce

3 eggs, divided

2 tablespoons chopped fresh parsley leaves

2 tablespoons lemon juice (about ½ lemon)

Salt and freshly ground pepper

½ cup all-purpose flour

¼ cup water

1½ cups canola oil

SPICY AIOLI:

Whisk together the mayonnaise, sour cream, hot sauce, and lemon juice in a bowl. Set aside until ready to use.

CRAB CAKES:

1. Set the crabmeat in a colander and press down on it to drain out excess liquid. In a medium bowl, add the crabmeat, 1 cup of the toasted bread crumbs, mayonnaise, mustard, hot sauce, 1 egg, parsley, lemon juice, and salt and pepper to taste, and gently combine. Divide the crab mixture into 8 equal patties, about ⅓ cup each, and arrange on a baking sheet lined with waxed paper.

2. Set up a breading station using 3 baking pans or pie plates. In the first dish, combine the flour with a healthy pinch of salt and pepper. In the second dish, whisk together the remaining 2 eggs with ¼ cup of water. In the third dish, combine the remaining bread crumbs with a healthy pinch of salt and pepper. Dredge the crab cakes in the seasoned flour, then in the egg wash, and then coat them thoroughly in the bread crumbs. Arrange on a baking sheet.

3. Line a plate with paper towels; set aside. Heat the canola oil in a large skillet over medium-high heat. Fry the cakes in batches of 4 until brown and crispy, about 3 minutes per side. Remove to the paper towel-lined plate.

AVOCADO-CITRUS SALAD:

2 oranges, preferably Cara Cara
    (Navel can also be used)

1 lemon

1 tablespoon Champagne vinegar

1 tablespoon minced shallot

Salt and freshly ground pepper

⅓ cup extra-virgin olive oil

1 avocado

1 head frisée (also known as curly
    endive), light green parts only

Pickled onions and radishes, optional

BRIAN'S KITCHEN POINTER

I don't know if you've ever ended up with the dreaded "claws." That's when your hands get coated with multiple layers of egg, flour, and bread crumbs from the dunking and dredging. There is a solution: Simply designate one hand as the "wet" hand, and the other as the "dry" hand. Each handles only the dipping in those ingredients. That way, you don't get your hands so gloppy that you have to stop to wash them.

AVOCADO-CITRUS SALAD:

1. Use a zester to remove several pieces of rind from the oranges and lemon; place the rinds in a medium bowl.

2. Segment the oranges by slicing off their ends and standing them upright on a cutting board. Use a paring knife to cut away the skin and white pith to expose the fruit. Slice between the membranes to release each orange segment one by one. Cut the segments into ½-inch pieces and place in the medium bowl with the orange and lemon rinds. Squeeze 1 tablespoon juice from the remaining orange membrane into a small bowl.

3. To make the vinaigrette, add in the small bowl with the orange juice, 1 tablespoon lemon juice, the Champagne vinegar, shallot, a pinch of salt, and a few grinds of pepper. Let sit to macerate for 10 minutes. Whisk in the olive oil. Season with salt and pepper to taste, and set aside.

4. Slice the avocado lengthwise into two halves. Remove the pit and peel, and slice the flesh into ½-inch pieces. Place in the bowl with the orange pieces, season with salt and pepper, add a spoonful or two of the lemon-Champagne vinaigrette, and toss gently so as not to break the fruits.

5. Add the frisée and, if you choose, the pickled onions and radishes, to the orange and avocado. Season with salt and pepper and just enough dressing to coat. Add more salt and pepper to taste.

6. To assemble, evenly divide the salad among 4 plates. Place 2 crab cakes on each plate next to the salad. Top each cake with aioli.

REMOULADE:

Make the remoulade by whisking together ½ cup mayonnaise, 2 tablespoons sweet chili sauce, and 1 tablespoon bottled lemon juice in a small bowl. Add salt and pepper to taste.

SEARED SCALLOPS *with* CREAMLESS CREAMED CORN *and* BACON LARDONS

I think its funny to have a favorite scallop memory . . . but I do. I was filming a television show with live musical guest Andrea Bocelli who was accompanied by Mario Reyes of Gipsy Kings fame. We were rehearsing in Bridgeport, Connecticut, and the night before the show, the cast went out to dinner at a local Italian restaurant. The courses of food just kept coming . . . antipasti, bruschetta, and pasta. My favorite was the scallop course. They were seared with a nice crunchy brown exterior and had a very delicate lemon garlic herb flavor. I think Andrea and Mario must have liked it too because Mario started serenading the restaurant with an original song he had written for Andrea. That restaurant got a great unexpected show that evening, and I got a great food memory complete with a vocal and guitar soundtrack.

SERVES 4

CORN:

2 thick slices bacon (about 5 ounces total), cut into 1-by-¼-inch pieces

1 tablespoon unsalted butter

½ small white onion, finely chopped

Salt and freshly ground pepper

1 pound corn kernels (about 3 cups), fresh or frozen (kernels from about 4 ears corn)

1½ cups water

SCALLOPS:

3 tablespoons canola or vegetable oil

20 large sea scallops, patted dry

Salt and freshly ground pepper

4 tablespoons unsalted butter

2 tablespoons dry white wine

1 to 2 tablespoons fresh lemon juice

2 tablespoons chopped chives

1 tablespoon chopped fresh parsley leaves

1. Heat bacon in a large skillet over medium heat and cook until crisp and brown. Use a slotted spoon to transfer the bacon to a paper towel-lined plate; set aside. Pour off all but 1 tablespoon of the bacon fat and return the skillet to the stovetop. Add the butter. Once melted, add the onions, season with salt and pepper, and cook until translucent, 3 to 5 minutes. Add the corn, season with more salt and pepper, and cook until they start to crackle. Add the water and simmer until reduced to about ½ cup. Season to taste with salt and pepper.

2. Transfer three-fourths of the corn and its liquid to a blender (or use an immersion blender) and process to a chunky oatmeal consistency. Return to the skillet with the remaining whole kernels and warm through. If it's too thick, add some water; if it's too thin, let it reduce a bit. Season again as needed and set aside.

3. Heat oil in a large skillet over high heat. Season both sides of the scallops with salt and pepper. When the oil is hot, place the scallops one at a time into the pan. Sear scallops on first side until caramelized and crispy, about 4 minutes (avoid moving them or peeking as they will not crisp up as nicely.) Flip and cook on the second side for 30 to 60 seconds. Remove to plate. Set skillet aside to

Whenever possible, avoid scallops that have been treated with the preservative formula called "STP." (These scallops will be ghost white and will be coated in a gluey sauce.) Instead, shop around for "dry" scallops—fresh, untreated shellfish that will be a little pink in color. If you can only find treated scallops, rinse them thoroughly, then soak them for 15 minutes in a quart of water with a cup of lemon juice and a teaspoon of salt. Rinse and pat dry before cooking.

make sauce. (If you don't have a pan large enough to hold all 20 scallops, then cook them in two batches. You can hold the first batch in a low oven while the second batch cooks.)

4. Set the skillet used to cook the scallops back over medium heat and melt the butter. Stir until the butter solids start to brown. Stir in the wine. Add 1 tablespoon of the lemon juice. Taste and season with salt, pepper, and more lemon juice as needed. Add 1 tablespoon each of the chives and parsley. Keep warm.

5. Reheat corn. Line up four large plates. Evenly divide the corn between plates and sprinkle with reserved bacon pieces. Top each plate with 5 scallops. Drizzle a little pan sauce over the scallops. Top with chives and serve immediately.

SEAFOOD *and* FENNEL CIOPPINO

Italian fishermen invented this dish to cook all the odds and ends that were left over from the catches of the day. But I use cioppino a lot for entertaining. It's a one-pot preparation and can sit and stay warm until your guests are ready to eat, and then you can serve it steaming hot. (Make sure not to overcook the seafood or it will become tough and dried out.) My take on this dish includes fennel, which adds just the faintest hint of licorice to the traditional Italian flavors. The mix of ingredients creates an incredibly filling meal that you'll never want to stop eating. Fortunately, if you serve it with plenty of crusty artisanal bread, you can mop up every last drop.

SERVES 4

1 leek

3 tablespoons olive oil

1 large bulb fennel, sliced

4 large cloves garlic, minced

1 (28-ounce) can crushed tomatoes

5 cups fish stock

1 cup white wine

2 bay leaves

½ tablespoon dried basil

½ tablespoon dried oregano

½ teaspoon red pepper flakes

½ pint cherry tomatoes, cut in half

¾ pound mussels

1 pound cod or halibut, skin removed
    and cut into 2-inch pieces

¾ pound sea scallops

¾ pound shrimp, peeled and deveined

½ pound crabmeat

½ cup chopped parsley

Salt and freshly ground black pepper
    to taste

1. Thinly slice the white part of the leek and soak the slices in a bowl filled with cold water for 5 minutes. Drain and set aside (you may have to repeat if any grit remains on the leek).

2. Heat the olive oil in a large Dutch oven over medium heat. Add the leek and fennel and sauté for 3 minutes, or until translucent.

3. Add the garlic and sauté for another 2 minutes.

4. Add the crushed tomatoes, fish stock, white wine, bay leaves, basil, oregano, red pepper flakes, and cherry tomatoes. Cover and reduce the heat to low. Simmer for 45 minutes.

5. Add the seafood, starting with the mussels. Cook for about 3 minutes, or until the mussels open. Discard any opened mussels.

6. Add the cod and cook for 1 minute. Add the scallops and cook for 1 minute more, then add the shrimp and cook until it turns pink.

7. Add the crabmeat and parsley and stir to combine. Taste and add salt and pepper as desired. Serve in large bowls with crusty sourdough bread.

BRIAN'S KITCHEN POINTER

Make this an easy entertaining meal by making the broth a day early and keeping it in the refrigerator (or even earlier, and freezing it). Then, when it's time to serve, just reheat, add the seafood until cooked, and serve. You can also keep leftover cioppino in the refrigerator, covered, for up to 2 days with fish in it. It's just as good reheated!

SHRIMP *and* POLENTA

In Venice they call this dish *schie con polenta,* and they make it with the local small, gray, salty shrimp and a heavy dose of garlic. I make mine with larger shrimp, but I add garlic like a Venetian would. Polenta is a great go-to for a creamy base that allows other flavors to come through. I like this as a main course and in smaller portions that make an ideal appetizer. If you're in a hurry, you can substitute "quick cooking" polenta. If you want a smokier flavor, use bacon instead of pancetta.

SERVES 4

2 pounds extra-large shrimp, shelled and deveined, shells reserved

Salt

1½ cups polenta

½ cup light cream

2 tablespoons olive oil

¼ pound pancetta, diced

1 large yellow onion, chopped

Freshly ground black pepper to taste

3 cloves garlic, chopped

¼ teaspoon red pepper flakes

½ cup dry white wine

1 pint grape tomatoes, sliced in half

3 tablespoons chopped Italian flat-leaf parsley

2 tablespoons salted butter

1. Make the shrimp stock by boiling the reserved shrimp shells in a large pot with 6 cups of water. Reduce the heat and simmer for 10 minutes. Remove from heat, cool, and then strain the shells out of the stock. Discard the shells.

2. Bring the shrimp stock to a boil in a large pot. Season with a generous pinch of salt.

3. Slowly add the polenta in a thin stream, whisking constantly for 2 minutes. Reduce the heat to low and cook, stirring often with a wooden spoon, until the polenta is thickened and tender, about 35 minutes.

4. Add the cream and cook for 5 minutes more. The polenta should be thick but still have a pourable consistency. Taste and add salt as desired.

5. While the polenta is cooking, heat the olive oil in a large pan over medium heat. Add the pancetta and cook until crispy, about 6 to 8 minutes. Remove to a plate lined with a paper towel.

6. Increase the heat to medium-high. Generously season the shrimp with salt and pepper. Cook the shrimp for 2 minutes per side, or until pink and slightly brown on the edges. Remove to a plate.

7. Add the onions to the pan. Season with salt and pepper and cook for 5 minutes, or until soft and translucent.

8. Add the garlic and red pepper flakes and cook for 1 minute. Add the wine and tomatoes, bring to a simmer, and cook until the tomatoes release their juice and become tender.

9. Add the parsley, butter, and shrimp and cook until the shrimp are heated through, about 2 minutes. Stir in the pancetta. Taste and add salt and pepper as desired.

10. Spoon the polenta into 4 shallow pasta bowls and top with the shrimp mixture.

FABULOUS FISH DISHES

Oslo was all about the fish. Yes, there was a skating competition that brought me there in the first place, but that seemed almost like background. I think I must have had salmon for almost every meal. I ate the cured salmon called gravlax (served with dill—wow!), smoked salmon, salmon sushi, steamed salmon filets, and grilled salmon. I ate so much salmon that I'm pretty sure I'm good with omega-3 oils for the rest of my life.

And the fish didn't stop with the salmon. Oslo was the place I first tried pickled herring, and I have to say, it wasn't bad (then again, I'm a huge fan of anything pickled—except beets). Oslo was also an education in the many types of caviar. I know some people aren't big on caviar, and I used to be one of them. Now I think caviar is great just spooned on top of a toast point, but I especially like how the Norwegians (and the Russians, and the Latvians, and . . .) serve it—like a big ritual. They give you a stack of fresh blini—small potato pancakes—and a selection of fillings like chopped eggs and diced onions. You spoon a layer of sour cream on your blini, choose your fillings, and top with caviar.

My culinary experiences in Oslo drove home the point that the best way to cook and serve fish is fresh and simple, and sometimes with a bit of flair and a slight bit of decadence—like the Sea Bass with Roasted Cauliflower Puree and Leek Buerre Blanc (page 160). The mild taste of fish is usually the perfect foil for richer flavors, like butter, wine, and herbs. Every fish has its own distinct flavor, so try to mix it up and find your own mouthwatering combinations to serve.

SEARED HALIBUT *with* GRILLED TOMATO SAUCE *and* SAUTÉED ARTICHOKE HEARTS

Searing is one of the best ways to prepare a firm-bodied whitefish like this halibut, because it keeps it nice and moist without it falling apart. To inspire a good sear and create a nice golden crust, pat the halibut filet dry with a paper towel before you grill it. Almost any type of tomato (although I'm partial to heirloom)—and especially grilling the tomatoes—will complement the texture and understated flavor of the halibut. Grilling the tomatoes brings out a lot of their sweetness and adds a slightly charred smokiness to the dish. As an alternative, you can cook the tomatoes under a broiler, placed on a sheet pan, cut-side down, and broil until the skin is charred.

SERVES 4

SAUTÉED ARTICHOKE HEARTS:

4 artichokes

Salt and freshly ground pepper

¼ cup olive oil, divided

Juice of 1 lemon, divided

¼ pound pancetta, diced

½ medium yellow onion, diced

¼ teaspoon red pepper flakes

1½ cups frozen peas, thawed

2 sprigs thyme, leaves removed

SAUTÉED ARTICHOKE HEARTS:

1. Using a knife, cut 1 inch off the top and ½ inch off the stem of each artichoke. Peel the stem with a vegetable peeler.

2. Preheat oven to 425°F.

3. Tear off 4 large square pieces of heavy-duty foil. Place each artichoke into the center of each piece of foil. Sprinkle each with salt and pepper and drizzle with 2 tablespoons olive oil and half the lemon juice. Gather up the corners of the foil and press together on top to tightly seal the artichoke. You can wrap in a second piece of foil if you don't think you have a tight enough seal.

4. Place in a roasting pan and bake for 30 to 45 minutes or until stem is fork tender. Let it sit until cool enough to handle. Peel the leaves off the artichokes to get to the heart, and gently clean the furry center out of each heart with a spoon. Slice the hearts first in half, then into strips about ¼ inch thick. Set aside.

5. When ready to serve; heat remaining 2 tablespoons olive oil in a large skillet over medium low heat. Cook pancetta until crispy about 6 to 8 minutes. Remove pancetta with a slotted spoon to a plate lined with a paper towel. Turn heat up to medium and add onion and cook for 4 to 5 minutes until soften and translucent. Add red pepper flakes, peas, artichoke hearts, and thyme leaves. Cook until heated through. Add lemon juice and pancetta then taste. Season with salt and pepper if necessary.

GRILLED TOMATO SAUCE:

5 plum tomatoes

5 tablespoons olive oil, divided

Salt and fresh ground pepper

½ medium yellow onion, diced

2 cloves garlic, chopped

½ cup vegetable stock

HALIBUT:

3 tablespoons canola or vegetable oil

4 halibut filets, each filet about
⅓ pound each, skin and any
bones removed

Salt and freshly ground pepper

3 tablespoons butter

4 sprigs of thyme

GRILLED TOMATO SAUCE:

1. Preheat grill over medium heat.

2. Slice each tomato in half and brush the cut side with olive oil and season with salt and pepper. Brush grill grates with olive oil. Place on grill cut side down and grill for 3 to 4 minutes until slightly charred. Turn and grill for another 3 to 4 minutes until charred. Remove to plate and let sit until cool enough to handle. Remove the skin and roughly chop. Set aside.

3. Heat remaining 2 tablespoons of olive oil in a medium saucepot over medium heat. Add onions and cook until translucent and softened about 5 minutes. Add garlic and cook for 1 minute. Add chopped grilled tomatoes and could for 2 minutes until mixture starts to simmer. Transfer to a blender and puree. Taste and season with salt and pepper if necessary. If sauce is too thick add vegetable stock. The sauce should be thick but have a pourable consistency. Pour back into saucepot and set aside. Reheat before serving with halibut.

HALIBUT:

1. Heat oil in a large heavy bottomed skilled over high heat. Season each filet liberally with salt and pepper. Sear the filets until brown and crispy about 3 to 4 minutes turn over and cook the other side, about 2 to 3 minutes. Reduce heat to low, add butter and 4 thyme sprigs. Using a spoon, baste the fillets with the melted butter and cook another minute. Hold in a low oven until ready to serve.

2. To assemble, line up 4 plates. On each plate lay a bed of the sautéed artichokes and peas. Top each with a piece of the halibut. Spoon the grilled tomatoes sauce around the plate and on top of the halibut. Serve immediately.

GRILLED SALMON *with* PEA-*and*-BASIL PESTO

One of my favorite ways to prepare salmon is to grill it. Sometimes I place it on a cedar plank, but most of the time it goes right on the grill. Both techniques give it a great smoky undertone. I added peas to the pesto to give the sauce a firmer texture, and this has become one of my go-to sauces. Whenever I would serve this to my opera-singing friend Lorenzo Malfatti, he would change the lyrics from famous Italian songs and arias to words related to the pea pesto topping. Instead of singing "O sole mio," it became "O peas in pesto." I make way more than I need and freeze the extra for use on white meat, pastas, and other fish. I use a cup of lemon verbena fresh from my garden, but if you can't lay your hands on the herb, feel free to substitute a tablespoon of lemon zest as directed below or ½ cup chopped fresh lemongrass. If you don't have pine nuts, substitute almonds.

SERVES 4

1 medium red potato, peeled

¼ cup pine nuts

3 cloves garlic

Pinch of red pepper flakes

2 cups frozen peas, thawed

2 cups basil leaves

½ cup Italian flat-leaf parsley

1 tablespoon lemon zest

Juice of 1 lemon

½ cup olive oil, plus 3 tablespoons

Salt and freshly ground black pepper to taste

4 salmon filets, about ⅓ pound each, skins removed

1. Boil the potato in a small pot of salted water. Cook until tender, about 10 minutes. Strain, let cool, and chop coarsely.

2. Toast the pine nuts in a dry skillet over medium-low heat, tossing occasionally, until the nuts are lightly browned and aromatic, about 3 to 5 minutes. Let cool.

3. Combine the pine nuts, garlic, and red pepper flakes in a food processor with the blade attachment. Pulse until finely chopped.

4. Add the potato, peas, basil, parsley, lemon zest, and lemon juice. With the processor running, slowly pour in ½ cup olive oil, blending until the mixture is smooth. Taste and add salt and pepper as desired. Set aside.

5. Brush the grill grate with olive oil and preheat on medium-high.

6. Brush both sides of the salmon filets with olive oil and coat with a layer of salt and pepper.

7. Grill the salmon for about 4 to 5 minutes. Flip the filets carefully, cover the grill, and grill for 3 to 4 minutes more.

8. Spoon a small amount of the pesto into the center of each plate and spread it out in a little round pool. Place a salmon filet on top of the pesto. Top each filet with a tablespoon of the pesto and serve immediately.

SEA BASS *with* ROASTED CAULIFLOWER PUREE *and* LEEK BUERRE BLANC

This cauliflower puree is a perfect substitute for anyone who likes mashed potatoes but is on a low-carb diet. I served this at a charity dinner, and when I sat down, the woman next to me said she had just lost sixty pounds by giving up carbs. She said she loved potatoes and was so upset that she couldn't eat these (pointing to the plate). She could not have been more excited to discover that it was cauliflower puree. When I saw her about a month later, she had lost even more weight and said she uses the cauliflower recipe all the time. The sweetness and tartness of the apples add so much flavor to the cauliflower, and when you roast them, they get browned and charred bits that make a wonderful caramel color. Process the puree chunky or smooth depending on whether you're going a little rustic or aiming for a more refined dish.

SERVES 4

ROASTED CAULIFLOWER PUREE:

1 head cauliflower, florets and stems cut into large pieces

1 Fuji apple, peeled, cored, and sliced

3 tablespoons olive oil

Salt and freshly ground black pepper

1½ cups vegetable stock or broth

LEEK BEURRE BLANC SAUCE:

1 large leek

2 tablespoons olive oil

Salt and freshly ground black pepper

1½ cups white wine

1 cup vegetable stock or broth

4 tablespoons cold butter

SEA BASS:

3 tablespoons canola oil

4 sea bass filets, about ⅓ of a pound a piece

Salt and freshly ground pepper

2 tablespoons butter

ROASTED CAULIFLOWER PUREE:

1. Preheat the oven to 400°F.

2. To a large baking dish add the cauliflower, apple, and 3 tablespoons olive oil. Season with salt and pepper, to taste, and toss to coat. Roast in oven until brown on top, about 25 minutes, then add the vegetable stock and roast until tender, another 20 minutes.

3. Add the roasted cauliflower, apple and stock to a food processor and puree until smooth. Transfer to a metal bowl and put over a pot of simmering water to keep warm.

LEEK BEURRE BLANC SAUCE:

1. Slice the green leaves off the leek and discard. Slice the stem into ¼-inch thick rings. Put them into a large bowl filled with cold water and let soak for 5 minutes. Remove the leeks and drain on a plate lined with paper towels.

2. Heat the olive oil in a large skillet over medium heat. Add leeks, season with salt and pepper to taste, and sauté until soft, about 4 minutes. Deglaze the pan with white wine and add the vegetable stock. Reduce by half and then whisk in the cold butter. Serve over sea bass.

SEA BASS:

1. Preheat oven to 325°F.

2. Heat canola oil in a large heavy bottomed skilled over high heat. Season each filet liberally with salt and pepper. Sear the filets until brown and crispy, turn over and crisp the other side, about 2 to 3 minutes per side.

Turn off the heat, add butter and, using a spoon, baste the filets with the melted butter. Transfer to the oven to finish cooking, about 3 to 4 minutes.

3. To plate, lay out 4 plates and spoon on about a ½ cup of the cauliflower puree, top with a piece of sea bass and drizzle with the leek sauce.

SEARED TUNA STEAK *with* GREEN GODDESS SAUCE *and* HEIRLOOM TOMATOES

You can't go wrong with a good seared fresh tuna steak. We have all come a long way from canned tuna. And it's just as quick and easy to sear this as it is to open a can of tuna. But really, the heart and soul of this dish is the Green Goddess sauce. Green Goddess is named for its tint, and it originated at the Palace Hotel in San Francisco in 1923. The hotel chef wanted to pay tribute to actor George Arliss and his hit play *The Green Goddess*. There are lots and lots of variations on this sauce, but this one is closer to a creamy chimichurri sauce. You can use it on fish, pork, chicken, or salads.

SERVES 4

1 bunch chives, chopped coarsely

3 scallions, chopped coarsely

½ cup fresh Italian flat-leaf parsley leaves, loosely packed

¼ cup fresh tarragon leaves, loosely packed

2 cloves garlic

1 tablespoon capers

2 anchovy filets

1 tablespoon Dijon mustard

1 teaspoon white wine vinegar

Zest of 1 lemon

2 tablespoons plain yogurt

¼ cup olive oil

Salt and freshly ground black pepper to taste

6 tablespoons olive oil, divided

4 tuna steaks, about ⅓ pound each (minimum 1-inch thick)

2 large heirloom tomatoes, diced

1. To create the Green Goddess sauce, blend all the ingredients except the olive oil, tuna steaks, and tomatoes in a blender until smooth. Taste and add more salt and pepper as desired. Refrigerate until ready to serve.

2. Toss the tomatoes in a medium bowl with 3 tablespoons olive oil, and salt and pepper to taste. Set aside.

3. Heat remaining 3 tablespoons olive oil in a large skillet over high heat. Generously season both sides of the tuna steaks with salt and pepper.

4. Sear the steaks on each side for 2–3 minutes. The tuna should be cooked to medium-rare and still pink inside.

5. Place a tuna steak on each plate and cover each steak with the heirloom tomatoes. Add a small dollop of Green Goddess sauce over the tomatoes and serve.

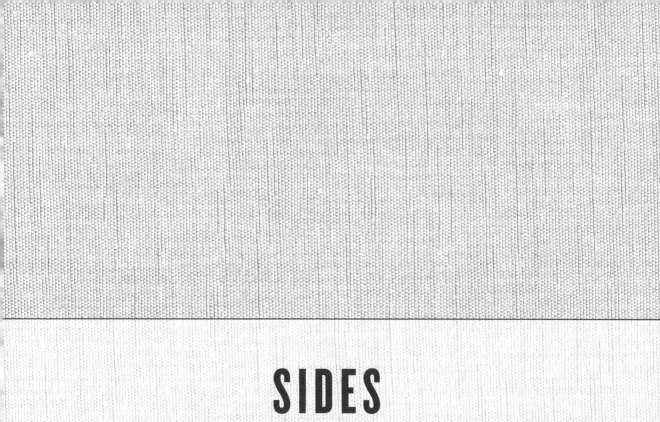

SIDES

THE COMBINATION OF A GREAT MAIN DISH AND SIDE DISH can make for a memorable meal, and, in fact, many side dishes can also be the unsung heroes of a meal. I remember when I sat down to eat at a skating competition banquet in The Hague, Netherlands, I had a remarkably tasty complement to my main course. Usually, these banquets are seriously rubber-chicken affairs! That night, the main course arrived with an upside-down funnel of what looked like pudding. I thought, "Wow, they put dessert on the same plate as the main course." Being the dessert fiend that I am, I, of course, went right for it.

I was totally surprised at the nutty taste and velvety consistency. It had a slightly grassy flavor, and when I checked the menu to find out what it was, I discovered it was not dessert, but a parsnip puree. It was a fairly simple side dish, but between the interesting shape and the great blend of flavors, that side dish stuck with me long after I forgot the main course. That's the mark of a fantastic accompaniment.

Rustle up your own parsnip side with my Mashed Parsnips and Celery Root (opposite). A side like this is great dinner-party fare because of its unexpected and fresh flavor combinations. For a side that is meant to be a hearty, filling addition to a more laid-back meal—or just a meal on its own—try my take on a casual classic comfort food, Mac and Cheese with Crunchy Topping (page 178).

ELEGANT ADDITIONS

For many years I produced and skated in a televised holiday skating special at the Mandalay Bay hotel in Las Vegas. I looked forward to that every year because it was a chance to have total creative control and really produce a memorable ice-skating show. But I also looked forward to it because Mandalay Bay is known for its elegance and its stunning array of restaurants. Finding a great meal of truly innovative dishes isn't hard at Mandalay Bay. The tough part is choosing which cuisine you want.

One year my friend and celebrated actress, Judith Light, came to meet me after the show with her husband, Robert, and our two friends Herb and Jonathan. Judith and Robert are great cooks and really fun people who love to explore good food, so we decided to try out the famous China Grill. China Grill is known for its unique interpretation of classic Asian cuisine, and the restaurant didn't disappoint.

We had an incredible meal, but what really blew me away was a super-stylish side dish—Lobster Mashed Potatoes. If you're like me, that's not a food combination that comes first to mind.

As a matter of fact, the two seem at opposite ends of the great spectrum of food. But, man, eat Lobster Mashed Potatoes and you'll never want plain mashed potatoes again. And the dish was beautifully colored—a cross between saffron and tangerine. That's the type of presentation and surprising flavor combination I captured in the Blue Cheese–Stuffed Tomatoes on page 168. So just keep in mind that refined sides can receive a lot of attention while still allowing the main course to shine.

MASHED PARSNIPS *and* CELERY ROOT

Sometimes you just need a really nice side dish that can be a reliable background to the main course but still has subtle, interesting flavors. This side does just that, and it works as a nice meal addition when you need a little something for the vegetarian at your dinner party. It makes an ideal bed for a protein like pork medallions or a sautéed chicken breast. And, just like the Roasted Cauliflower Puree on page 160, it's an excellent substitute for mashed potatoes for anyone who's looking to cut out carbs.

SERVES 4

1 large or 2 small parsnips, peeled and chopped

1 celery root, peeled and chopped

3 cups whole milk

1 tablespoon butter

Salt and freshly ground black pepper to taste

1. Cover the parsnips and celery root with the milk in a medium pot. Bring to a simmer and cook until the vegetables are tender and cooked through, about 30 minutes.

2. Strain the vegetables, reserving 1 cup of the milk.

3. Return the vegetables to the pot, add the butter, and mash with a potato masher. (For a smoother texture, blend in a food processor.)

4. Add the reserved milk. Season with salt and pepper to taste and stir well to incorporate. Serve in individual bowls.

BLUE CHEESE-STUFFED TOMATOES

One of the things that I like about serving these tomatoes is that they are not only handsome on the plate, but also completely self-contained and can be served in little individual portions to be set in front of each guest. You can easily turn this into a main course as well by adding half a pound of ground turkey sautéed with onion and serving it with a simple green salad. Either way, they are crammed with flavor from the crunchy pancetta and blue cheese.

SERVES 4

4 slices pancetta, diced

1 small yellow onion, diced

2 cloves garlic, chopped

¼ cup chopped walnuts

⅓ cup panko bread crumbs

Freshly ground black pepper to taste

½ cup crumbled blue cheese

2 tablespoons chopped fresh parsley

6 basil leaves, chopped

4 large plum tomatoes

Salt

2 tablespoons olive oil

1. Cook the pancetta in a large skillet over medium heat until brown and crispy. Remove to a plate lined with a paper towel.

2. Add the onions to the skillet and cook for 3 to 4 minutes, until slightly softened. Add the garlic, walnuts, and bread crumbs, season with pepper, and cook for 2 minutes. Remove from heat and let cool.

3. Once the mixture is cool, stir in the blue cheese, parsley, basil, and pancetta.

4. Preheat the oven to 425°F.

5. Slice the tomatoes in half lengthwise. Scoop out the pulp and seeds and discard. Place the tomato halves cut-side up on a baking sheet. Season with salt and pepper.

6. Fill each tomato half with the blue cheese mixture. Drizzle with olive oil and bake for about 8 minutes, or until lightly brown and toasted on top.

NAPA CABBAGE *with* GINGER *and* SESAME OIL STIR-FRY

I find that people really miss out on the interesting alternative cabbage offers to other greens. In a dish like this, the cabbage wilts slightly but retains a tiny bit of satisfying crunch. Napa cabbage offers a flavor that's full-bodied without being overwhelming, and it's perfectly suited for blending with the snappy citrus and vinegar tones of this classic stir fry. Fast to make, simple to prepare, it only takes a few minutes from refrigerator to table, and it brings an exciting mix of delicately balanced spices that will have your dinner guests rethinking their position on cabbage!

SERVES 4

3 tablespoons canola oil

1 small yellow onion, sliced

2 cloves garlic, chopped fine

2 teaspoons finely chopped fresh ginger

2 tablespoons soy sauce

1 tablespoon rice wine vinegar

1 tablespoon orange juice

1 small head Napa cabbage (1¼ to 1½ pounds), shredded or sliced thin

Pinch of red pepper flakes

2 teaspoons toasted sesame oil

1 tablespoon sesame seeds

1. Heat the canola oil in a large skillet over medium heat and sauté the onions for 3 to 4 minutes, or until soft.

2. Add the garlic and ginger and cook, stirring, for about 1 minute (don't let the garlic burn).

3. Reduce the heat and add the soy sauce, vinegar, and orange juice. Cook for about 5 minutes, or until the liquid has reduced by two-thirds.

4. Add the cabbage, increase heat to medium-high, and sauté for about 3 minutes. Stir frequently and cook until the cabbage is slightly wilted.

5. Stir in the red pepper flakes and sauté for 2 minutes more. Remove the pan from the heat. Stir in the sesame oil and half of the sesame seeds and toss to mix. Transfer to a serving bowl and sprinkle with the remaining sesame seeds.

BRIAN'S KITCHEN POINTER

One of the great things about using cabbage in a recipe is that there are many types that are virtually interchangeable. For instance, if you can't find the Napa cabbage for this recipe, you can just slip green cabbage in its place. You can also use bok choy for a slightly more peppery flavor, or savoy for a mild, sweeter flavor. Regardless, you'll be choosing a leafy green with sky-high levels of vitamin C and tons of fiber.

SPICY SNAP PEAS TWO WAYS

Speed is often of the essence when you need to get a side onto the plate without letting the entree cool. That's why I use this recipe all the time: It's a speedy side dish that doesn't sacrifice flavor. You can serve it several ways —all 'italiana with the traditional flavors of olive oil and Parmesan, or Asian style with spicy ginger and chile paste—or make up your own seasoning. However you make it, this is one of the easiest side dishes to prepare—the longest part of the preparation is waiting for the water to boil for the blanching! If you're not partial to snap peas, sub in your favorite type of green beans.

SERVES 4

ITALIAN STYLE:

3 tablespoons olive oil

¾ teaspoon red pepper flakes
(¼ teaspoon if you prefer mild)

2 cloves garlic, smashed

1 pound sugar snap peas, blanched

Salt and freshly ground black pepper
to taste

3 tablespoons grated Parmesan

ASIAN STYLE:

3 tablespoons canola oil

1 tablespoon Thai red chile paste

1 teaspoon grated fresh ginger

1 teaspoon chopped garlic

3 tablespoons soy sauce

1 pound sugar snap peas, blanched

1 tablespoon sesame seeds

ITALIAN STYLE:

1. Heat the olive oil in a large skillet over medium-low heat. Add the red pepper flakes and garlic and cook until the garlic begins to brown, about 3 to 4 minutes.

2. Increase the heat to medium. Add the peas, season with salt and pepper, and toss to coat. Cook until the peas are heated through, about 2 to 3 minutes.

3. Remove from the heat, add the Parmesan, and toss to coat. Transfer to a serving bowl and serve.

ASIAN STYLE:

1. Heat the canola oil in a large skillet over medium heat. Add the chile paste and mix to break up the paste and blend it into the oil.

2. Add the ginger and garlic and cook until the garlic begins to brown, about 1 to 2 minutes.

3. Increase the heat to medium-high. Add the soy sauce and peas, toss to coat, and cook until the peas are heated through, about 2 to 3 minutes.

4. Add the sesame seeds and toss to coat. Transfer to a serving bowl and serve.

HEARTY SIDEKICKS

Through my skating, I was able to experience Russia before the breakup of the Soviet Union. In 1986, when I slipped behind the Iron Curtain to compete in the Goodwill Games in Moscow, it seemed like a place right out of a spy novel. The Berlin Wall was still standing back then, and Russia was known as the USSR. It was an intimidating experience to travel in that country. You had the impression that you were being watched all the time. I became used to seeing the women sitting behind tiny desks on each floor of the hotel, whose only job was to monitor the hallways. (I used to look out my peephole every once in a while to see if they were listening at my door.) But what really got to me was the dismal food. After having chicken soup in my hotel that was basically warm, gray water with a chicken bone or two floating in it (not kidding), I sort of gave up hope of finding a good meal during the competition.

Fortunately, I had a friend in town. All through the eighties, Russian skater Alexander Fadeev and I were neck and neck at almost every competition. He won the World Championships in 1985 and I won them in 1986 and '88. We were pretty fierce competitors. But a funny thing happened on the run up to the 1988 Olympics: He and I became good friends.

Alexander wanted to show me around while I was in town. As a local, he knew a few little hole-in-the-wall restaurants that served real, honest-to-goodness traditional Russian food. These were places you weren't going to find in any guidebook, and where I probably

wasn't even allowed to go. But Alexander didn't mind bending the rules, and that's how we wound up in a family-owned cafe off an alley in the far reaches of Moscow. In the meal we shared there, one dish stood out. It was a version of the classic Russian side dish, pelmini. Pelmini is a heavy dumpling made out of a simple dough of flour, water, and eggs. The pelmini we had that night were filled with shredded beef and covered not with the traditional dollop of sour cream, but with a delicious, rich cheese sauce. I can still taste it now, and I think of it whenever I make my version of mac and cheese with three different types of cheese and a super-crunchy topping (page 178).

OLIVE-*and*-HERB RED POTATOES

This side dish works just as well with chicken or fish as it does with meat. Or serve it by itself vegetarian style, paired with a salad. It is easy to change up the seasonings to suit your own preferences. Go heavy on the garlic, or use sage in place of the rosemary for an entirely different flavor. This side dish is easy and quick to pull together—which makes it ideal for a meal with lots of other moving parts, or if you're in a hurry. When I have the larger family group to feed, I just double, triple, or quadruple the recipe.

SERVES 4

1½ pounds small red potatoes, quartered

¼ cup olive oil

1 tablespoon red wine vinegar

1 teaspoon finely chopped fresh thyme leaves

1 teaspoon finely chopped fresh rosemary leaves

2 tablespoons chopped fresh Italian flat-leaf parsley

¼ teaspoon red pepper flakes

¼ cup finely chopped pitted mixed olives

Salt and freshly ground black pepper to taste

1. Boil the potatoes in a large pot of salted water for 6 to 8 minutes, or until tender but still firm enough to hold their shape and not fall apart. Drain and return the potatoes to the pot set over low heat.

2. While the potatoes are boiling, whisk together the olive oil, vinegar, herbs, red pepper flakes, and olives in a large bowl. Season with salt and pepper to taste.

3. Add the dressing to the cooked potatoes in the pot and toss until completely coated. Serve warm.

BUTTERNUT SQUASH *and* GOAT CHEESE GRATIN

This is my sister Jill's recipe for gratin with a few tweaks here and there. She has seven kids, so she knows what she is doing. The subtle sweetness of the squash works with the tangy nature of the goat cheese. It's a great alternative for anyone trying to dodge carbs and up the veggies in their diet. It's also a cinch to make and the perfect potluck dish. Jill serves this at all her kids' high school graduation parties (she's up to six, one more to go). You can even make it the day before and store it in the refrigerator under plastic wrap. Thanks, Jill.

SERVES 4

1 butternut squash

Salt and freshly ground pepper

½ pound goat cheese, crumbled

½ cup vegetable broth

¼ cup olive oil, divided

1 tablespoon butter

2 cloves garlic, smashed

1½ cups fresh bread crumbs (see Kitchen Pointer below)

¼ cup grated Parmesan

BRIAN'S KITCHEN POINTER

If you can't find fresh bread crumbs, you can quickly make your own. Just cut about a quarter of a loaf of crusty Italian bread into small cubes. Place the cubes in a food processor fitted with the blade attachment, and pulse until coarse.

1. Preheat the oven to 400°F. Brush an 8 × 11-inch baking dish with olive oil.

2. Cut off ½ inch from the top and bottom of the squash. Peel the squash, cut in half lengthwise, and seed. Cut each half in half lengthwise.

3. Set up a food processor with the slicing attachment. If you do not have a food processor, slice the squash into ¼-inch-thick slices with a knife or mandoline. Slice each quarter of the squash in the food processor. Once the processor bowl is full, remove the slices to a sheet tray or bowl. You may have to slice the squash in batches.

4. Place a layer of sliced squash into the bottom of the baking dish. Season with salt and pepper and sprinkle with about a quarter of the goat cheese. Repeat process until all the squash and goat cheese have been used. Pour in the vegetable broth and drizzle top with 2 tablespoons of olive oil.

5. Heat the remaining 2 tablespoons of olive oil with the butter in a large skillet over medium-low heat. Add the garlic and cook for 2 to 3 minutes until the garlic begins to brown. Remove the garlic and discard. Add the bread crumbs to the skillet and toss until they are completely coated with the butter mixture. Remove from the heat and mix in the Parmesan. Sprinkle the bread crumb mixture over the top of the gratin.

6. Cover loosely with foil and bake for 25 minutes. Remove foil and bake an additional 10 to 15 minutes until the squash is fork tender and the top is golden brown. Let rest for 5 minutes before serving.

MAC *and* CHEESE *with* CRUNCHY TOPPING

It's hard to find someone who doesn't love mac and cheese. To me, it's the ultimate comfort food. My twist on this classic uses three distinctly different cheeses. The Asiago brings a rich nutty flavor, the Fontina is subtler and adds some sweetness, and the Gouda adds a bit of bite. The three melt together into a really creamy texture that coats the pasta and contrasts with the crunchy, garlicky bread crumb topping. I like to serve this when family comes to The Shack (our beach house). I have a lot of nieces and nephews to feed, and it has become a tradition.

SERVES 4

1 pound orecchiette pasta

2 tablespoons olive oil

2 tablespoons all-purpose flour

1¾ cups whole milk, at room temperature

¼ pound Asiago cheese, shredded

¼ pound Fontina cheese, shredded

¼ pound Gouda cheese, shredded

½ teaspoon ground white pepper

Salt to taste

2 tablespoons butter

2 cloves garlic, chopped fine

1 tablespoon freshly chopped parsley leaves

2 cups fresh bread crumbs, toasted

¼ cup grated Parmesan

1. Bring a large pot of salted water to a boil over high heat. Add the pasta and cook until al dente, about 8 minutes.

2. While the pasta is cooking, add the olive oil to a saucepan over medium heat. Whisk in the flour, stirring constantly for 2 minutes.

3. Slowly add the milk, whisking well to get rid of all the lumps, and bring to a simmer. Stir in the cheeses, season with the white pepper, and salt to taste.

4. Drain the pasta and return it to the pot. Pour the cheese sauce over the pasta and stir to combine.

5. Melt the butter in a large skillet over medium-low heat. Add the garlic and cook for 2 minutes. Add the parsley, bread crumbs, and Parmesan and mix until the bread crumbs are completely coated with the butter mixture.

6. Serve the pasta and cheese in small bowls topped with the bread crumb mixture.

PARMESAN-CRUSTED BRUSSELS SPROUTS

When my friend Yvonne took a few bites of this side dish and asked me how I had prepared the artichoke hearts, I had to explain that they were actually brussels sprouts. She said, "Oh, I don't eat brussels sprouts." Then she finished off the rest of them. I don't blame her. These brussels sprouts are crunchy, salty, cheesy, and tender all at the same time. This is a sturdy, rich side that can be paired with other hearty dishes, like Short Rib Bourguignon (page 118) or Spanish Chicken with Peppers and Olives (page 137).

SERVES 4

1 pound brussels sprouts

½ cup olive oil, plus 2 tablespoons, divided

Salt and freshly ground black pepper

½ cup all-purpose flour

1 large egg

1¼ cups panko bread crumbs

⅓ cup Parmesan

1 teaspoon paprika

2 tablespoons chopped fresh parsley

6 basil leaves, chopped

½ lemon, cut into 4 wedges

1. Preheat the oven to 400°F.

2. Cut the stem ends off the brussels sprouts and remove any spotted or yellowed leaves. Cut each sprout in half.

3. Place the brussels sprouts in a 9 × 13-inch baking dish. Drizzle with 2 tablespoons of olive oil and lightly season with salt and pepper.

4. Roast for about 20 to 25 minutes or until slightly tender. Remove and let cool completely.

5. Place 3 large shallow bowls side by side. Place the flour in the first bowl, whisk together the egg with ¼ cup water in the second bowl, and mix the bread crumbs, Parmesan, paprika, parsley, and remaining salt and pepper in the third bowl.

6. Working in batches, lightly dredge the brussels sprouts in the flour and shake off any excess, then coat them in the egg wash and dredge in the bread crumb mixture. Place on a baking sheet.

7. Heat ½ cup of olive oil in a large skillet over medium heat. Fry the brussels sprouts in batches until golden brown, about 2 minutes per side. Remove to a plate lined with a paper towel.

8. Transfer the brussels sprouts to a serving platter, garnish with chopped basil, and serve with lemon wedges on the side.

ROASTED WINTER VEGETABLES

Simple, quick, and a snap to make, what's not to love about this side dish? It combines sturdy flavors and textures with mega amounts of nutrients, and it is the perfect complement to chicken, cold-water fish, and meats of all types. I especially love how this side looks on the plate: a medley of colors led by the beautiful skin of the squash. These vegetables are great the next day; you can even add them to spaghetti with just a little Parmesan and olive oil.

SERVES 4

1 small acorn squash

1 pint brussels sprouts, sliced in half

¾ pound small red potatoes, quartered

1 (6-ounce) bag frozen pearl onions, thawed

5 sprigs fresh thyme

¼ cup olive oil

Salt and freshly ground black pepper to taste

4 ounces baby portobello (also called cremini) mushrooms (6 to 8 mushrooms), stemmed and halved

1. Preheat the oven to 425°F.

2. Slice the squash in half from top to bottom. Remove and discard the seeds. Put the squash halves on a cutting board, cut-side down, and cut each into ½-inch-thick slices. Transfer the slices to a large bowl.

3. Combine the brussels sprouts, potatoes, pearl onions, and thyme with the squash in the bowl. Add the olive oil, season with salt and pepper, and toss to coat.

4. Spread the vegetables on 2 baking sheets in single layers and roast for 35 to 40 minutes. Add the mushrooms and roast for 10 minutes longer, or until tender.

5. Transfer and serve in a bowl or on a platter.

SWEETS

IF LOVING DESSERTS WERE A CRIME, I'D BE SERVING LIFE IN PRISON. In fact, one of my favorite dessert memories happened when I was just a little kid. I was training at my local rink and the figure-skating club had invited Dorothy Hamill to skate in our annual club show. She hadn't yet won Olympic gold, but she was the Junior National Champion, and after meeting her, I wound up following her career from then on.

After the show practice, we all went out to a local restaurant named Farrell's. The place was decorated to look "old-timey," like an 1890s candy store. And there actually was a whole alley by the cash register that was covered floor to ceiling with different types of candies, like dots on paper strips and root beer stick candy in glass apothecary jars.

But the best thing about Farrell's was the ridiculously huge ice-cream sundae for large groups, called "The Zoo." It required two waiters to carry it out on a litter, and every time one was ordered, bells and sirens would go off. The guys carrying The Zoo would run around the restaurant like crazy, finally stopping at the right table. The single-serving version of The Zoo was called "The Trough." It was gigantic, and if you managed to finish it off, you got a pin-on button that said "I made a pig of myself at Farrell's." (I still have mine somewhere!)

That day, we told the waiter that it was Dorothy's birthday. We knew that if you went to Farrell's on your birthday, you got a free sundae and an extra helping of embarrassment because they made you stand on a chair while the whole staff (and most of the restaurant) sang "Happy Birthday to You." Nowadays I keep my portions smaller, but I still do love desserts.

CHOCOLATE TEMPTATIONS

My greatest chocolate quest took place in Helsinki, the capital of Finland. I was nineteen years old, competing in the World Championships for the first time. I couldn't believe how beautiful the city was, with its stately old buildings and trams running along overhead power lines. When I wasn't skating, I went exploring. One day I came across a Fazer chocolate shop—they're famous throughout Scandinavia and Europe, but they were new to me.

The shop was like something out of Willy Wonka. The windows were filled with the most fantastic chocolate creations. It was just before Easter, and the displays were amazing. They had big sugar eggs with intricate scenes inside and hand-painted papier-mâché eggs concealing small toys. The chocolate bunny sculptures were so detailed, they must have been done by a chocolate Michelangelo. I remember the baskets wrapped in beautiful embossed foils and all different colors of cellophane. It was an Easter wonderland.

My absolute favorite things in the store were their "Easter Eggs." They looked like regular white eggs, but the egg had been removed from the shell through a tiny pinprick, the inside had been cleaned, and then the shell was filled with pure, solid chocolate!

TARTUFO

My friend Mike has a very odd favorite dessert that served as the inspiration for my tartufo: He crumbles cookies into a glass of milk, throws in a couple scoops of ice cream, and eats the whole concoction with a spoon. I thought he needed a massive upgrade, so I made this tartufo for him on an episode of my show. It's a simple dessert that even Mike can make. You can prepare this dessert days in advance and store it in the freezer wrapped tightly in plastic. That makes it ideal for a quick dessert to cap off your next dinner party.

SERVES 4

¾ cup crushed chocolate cookies

½ cup chopped bittersweet chocolate (recommended: Ghirardelli 70%)

1 pint vanilla ice cream

4 brandied or maraschino cherries

½ cup granulated sugar

⅓ cup heavy cream

1 teaspoon vanilla extract

½ teaspoon salt

4 sprigs mint

1. Combine the cookie crumbs and chocolate pieces in a large resealable bag.

2. Using a large round ice-cream scoop, scoop out a ball of ice cream and leave it in the ice cream scoop. Poke a hole in the center of the ball with the handle of a wooden spoon. Push a cherry into the hole, then cover the hole with a bit of ice cream.

3. Put the ball of ice cream into the bag of cookies and chocolate pieces. Shake it around, pressing gently to completely coat the ice cream.

4. Remove the coated ice-cream ball and put it on a tray. Repeat to make 4 ice-cream balls. Place in the freezer, covered, for 30 minutes.

5. About 10 minutes before serving, combine the sugar with ¼ cup of water in a heavy saucepan over medium-high heat. Bring to a simmer and cook until the mixture turns a deep golden brown.

6. Remove from the heat and carefully whisk in the heavy cream, vanilla extract, and salt. Set aside to cool to room temperature.

7. When you're ready to serve, divide the caramel sauce among 4 plates. Remove the tartufos from the freezer and slice them in half. Arrange 2 halves on each plate and garnish with mint sprigs.

THE SECRET BEHIND THE DESSERT

My friend Mike Weiss's creation that inspired my tartufo should, according to him, be given respect. In Mike's words: "It is not a concoction. It is a state-of-the-art cuisine that was only taught in the late seventeenth century to eight Parisian Mennonites, and has lived on only through passing down from generations in the Weiss family. Some say, six lost their lives protecting the recipe from getting into the wrong hands. With that, you have been chosen by a board of five remaining protectors to learn the secret. With great power comes great responsibility."

SERVES 1 HUNGRY BOY

1 (24-ounce) glass
3 oversize scoops Breyers vanilla ice cream
As many Oreos as it takes
1 full cup nonfat skim milk

1. Put ice cream in glass. Chop ice cream minimally with a spoon, but still so thick it has to be eaten with a spoon.

2. Add one untwisted half of an Oreo cookie to your oversize spoon, then spoon out ice cream and milk at a 33.3/33.3/33.3 ratio of cookie/ice cream/milk and eat.

3. Repeat with each bite until completely stuffed, and unable to get up off the sofa without the assistance of a family member or a large dog.

MOLTEN CHOCOLATE CAKES
with RASPBERRY SAUCE

My sister Lynn rates all my chocolate desserts on the "Rumpus Room" scale. There was a restaurant in San Francisco where we used to go called the Rumpus Room, and though the restaurant is long gone, the memory of their molten chocolate cake endures. It really was the most fantastic chocolate cake I've ever had. Here is my updated version. It has a surprising airy structure similar to a soufflé, thick melted chocolate, and thin flavorful raspberry sauce. Lynn gives it a thumbs up, but I can't get her to admit it deserves a full Rumpus Room rating.

SERVES 8

CAKES:

12 ounces semisweet chocolate, chopped, divided

2 tablespoons heavy cream

½ cup sugar, plus 2 tablespoons for dusting ramekins

1 cup butter, cubed, plus 2 tablespoons for ramekins

4 whole eggs

4 egg yolks

2 tablespoons all-purpose flour

¼ teaspoon salt

1 teaspoon almond extract

CAKES:

1. To make the ganache, melt 4 ounces of the chocolate with the heavy cream over a double boiler. Stir until smooth and chill until firm enough to scoop, about 30 minutes.

2. Preheat the oven to 400°F and butter 8 (7-ounce) ramekins. Coat the inside with 2 tablespoons of the sugar, making sure to tap out the excess.

3. In a medium bowl combine the remaining chocolate with 1 cup of butter over a double boiler until melted, stirring occasionally. Remove from heat and cool to room temperature. In large bowl beat together the eggs, egg yolks and the remaining ½ cup of sugar until pale, thick and light. Sift the flour over top, and fold in the salt and almond extract. Fold in the cooled chocolate mixture until uniformly combined. Divide equally between the prepared ramekins.

4. Using a small scoop or tablespoon, form the chilled ganache into 8 balls.

5. Put 1 into the center of each ramekin and press down slightly to cover with the batter. (Cakes can be prepared to this point, covered and held in the refrigerator for a few hours until ready to bake.)

6. Arrange the ramekins on a baking sheet and bake until the tops look set, about 10 to 12 minutes. Remove from oven and carefully invert the ramekins onto serving plates.

SAUCE AND GARNISH:

1 pint fresh raspberries

2 tablespoons superfine sugar

1 tablespoon Kirsch, optional

FOR RASPBERRY SAUCE AND GARNISH:

1. Reserve 8 raspberries for garnish. Mash the remaining raspberries through a fine meshed sieve into a small bowl. Discard the seeds.

2. Add the 2 tablespoons of superfine sugar and the kirsch and whisk until the sugar is dissolved.

3. Garnish cakes with raspberry sauce and reserved raspberries and serve immediately.

CHOCOLATE ALMOND PANNA COTTA

Northern Italians claim this dessert as their own—panna cotta is Italian for "cooked cream." Although it is a simple blend of just a few ingredients, the texture is what separates panna cottas. The best I've eaten look sturdy on the plate or in the container but really just barely hold together, and their taste is creamy and light. Try garnishing your panna cotta with amaretti cookies, which are super light and crunchy cookies that have an intense almond flavor, crushed with a rolling pin in a resealable bag. If you want to dress up the presentation a little, serve individual panna cottas in espresso glasses rather than ramekins!

SERVES 6

2½ teaspoons powdered gelatin

2 tablespoons cold water

2¼ cups almond milk

1¾ cups heavy cream, divided

⅓ cup plus 2 tablespoons sugar

½ teaspoon salt

1 cup bittersweet chocolate, finely chopped or grated, about 4 ounces

1 teaspoon vanilla extract

3 tablespoons almond liqueur (recommended Amaretto)

¼ cup crushed amaretti cookies, for garnish

Special Equipment: 6 (6-ounce) ramekins

1. In a small bowl mix together the gelatin with water and set aside to soften.

2. In a medium pot combine almond milk, 1 cup heavy cream, ⅓ cup sugar and salt. Put over medium heat and heat until just before it reaches a simmer. Remove from the heat and whisk in the softened gelatin, chocolate, vanilla, and almond liqueur. Whisk until smooth and chocolate is completely incorporated.

3. Arrange six (6-ounce) ramekins on a baking sheet. Evenly divide the mixture between the ramekins. Cover with plastic wrap and refrigerate for at least 5 hours or overnight.

4. In a large cold bowl, combine the remaining ¾ cup of heavy cream and remaining sugar. Whip with a hand mixer until soft peaks form. Remove the panna cotta from the refrigerator and top each with a heaping tablespoon of the whipped cream. Sprinkle with crushed amaretti cookies and serve.

BRIAN'S KITCHEN POINTER

To save calories you can replace the heavy cream in the Panna Cotta with almond milk and skip the whipped cream garnish.

SPICY COFFEE BROWNIES

Some of my skating friends were on a tour a while back, and one day they called and jokingly said that they wanted me to send them some of the brownies they had seen me make on my cooking show. I knew they didn't really expect me to, but I wanted to surprise them with a care package. They flipped out when they received them the next day. Now they keep asking me to send them a package whenever they're on tour.

The thing that makes this brownie variation so special is the combination of chocolate and spicy heat. It's an unexpected blend that makes it close to impossible to stop at one brownie. You can make these even more special by sprinkling salt shards over the top while they're still warm. Your friends will be waiting by their mailboxes!

SERVES 12 (38 BROWNIES)

12 ounces semisweet chocolate, chopped

¾ cup (1½ sticks) unsalted butter, cut into cubes

2 teaspoons instant espresso powder

1¼ cups all-purpose flour

2 teaspoons ancho chili powder

½ teaspoon cayenne pepper

4 large whole eggs, room temperature

3 large egg yolks, room temperature

1 tablespoon vanilla extract

1 cup light brown sugar

¾ cup granulated sugar

BRIAN'S KITCHEN POINTER

Make these brownies in the mini-muffin tins, and the bite-size brownies will come out looking so neat. But if you don't have mini tins, never fear—use a 9 x 13-inch baking dish instead, baking the brownies for 25 minutes, or just until the center is set. Then cut them into the size you prefer.

1. Preheat the oven to 325°F. Spray 2 (24-count) mini-muffin tins with nonstick cooking spray.

2. Combine the chocolate, butter, and espresso powder in a double boiler and melt until smooth. Remove from the heat.

3. In a medium bowl whisk together the flour and the spices. In another small bowl whisk together the eggs, egg yolks, and vanilla. Set both aside.

4. Stir the sugars into the chocolate mixture until completely incorporated. (At this point the chocolate mixture should be warm but not hot.)

5. Add the eggs to the chocolate mixture and stir until combined. Fold in the flour mixture in 2 stages, being careful not to overmix.

6. Using a small ice-cream scoop, divide the batter into the mini-muffin tins. Tap the tins gently to level the batter. Bake for 15 minutes, until mostly set. (A toothpick will not come out completely clean.)

7. Remove the pan from the oven and transfer the brownies to a serving platter when cool enough to handle.

NOT FRUIT COCKTAIL!

My dad's idea of a vacation was to pile the whole family into a car and just head out. We might wind up at the Grand Canyon, Yosemite, or Tahoe. One time, we were driving to Southern California and we stopped in the town of Solvang. Solvang is right next to Santa Barbara, but it's in a world of its own. It was founded in the early 1900s by Danish immigrants, who created a little piece of Denmark right there in California. All the buildings were built in the old-fashioned Danish style that you might see on a postcard of Copenhagen. There's a windmill and a copy of the famous Little Mermaid statue and—most important—Danish bakeries.

Dad needed to pick up something at a drugstore and sent me to the pastry shop across the street. He told me to "pick up one for each of us." But I misheard and thought he said "one of each." They had a window display crammed full of delicious fruit pastries—cherry, apple, berry—so I just loaded up on the pastries. When he came back to pay for them, imagine his surprise to see a box full of one of everything in the window—twenty pastries! He just laughed and paid the lady. It didn't take us long to get through all of them either. The Bourbon Bacon Apple Tarts (opposite) are reminiscent of that trip and are inspired by my dad, who loves to drink bourbon and eat apple desserts.

BOURBON BACON APPLE TARTS

I made this recipe for one of my shows that was all about bacon. When I showed my manager the recipe, she said, "Bacon for dessert, that sounds so gross." Well, that was her tune until she tasted one. Now it's her favorite dessert ever. You get a bunch of flavors here . . . the tartness of the apple, the smokiness of the bourbon, and the saltiness of the bacon. An important element to this dessert is the topping—candied bacon. You might think bacon covered in sugar is an odd combination, but I have friends who ask me to make extra candied bacon!

SERVES 24 (2-INCH) TARTS

4 slices bacon, plus 2 cooked and crumbled

3 tablespoons raw sugar

1 sheet frozen puff pastry, thawed

3 Granny Smith apples, peeled, cored, and diced

Juice of 1 lemon

½ teaspoon ground cinnamon

2 tablespoons maple syrup

¼ cup bourbon, plus 1 tablespoon

3 tablespoons butter, room temperature

½ cup brown sugar

½ cup heavy cream

1 tablespoon powdered sugar

1. Preheat the oven to 400°F.

2. Place a baking rack on a baking sheet. Spray the rack with nonstick cooking spray and lay the 4 slices of bacon on the rack in a single layer. Sprinkle with half of the raw sugar.

3. Bake in the oven for 8 minutes. Flip the bacon and sprinkle with the remaining raw sugar. Return to the oven and bake until the bacon is browned and crisp, about 8 minutes.

4. Remove the bacon from the oven, transfer to a plate, and set it aside to cool completely. Once cool, break the candied bacon into small shards and reserve.

5. Unfold the puff pastry onto a lightly floured surface and roll the sheet out slightly. Cut out 24 rounds with a 2-inch biscuit cutter. Place the rounds on a baking sheet lined with parchment paper. Top with a baking rack to help keep the rounds uniform and even as they bake.

6. Bake in the oven until the rounds are golden brown, about 12 minutes. Remove and set aside to cool.

7. Toss the diced apples with the lemon juice in a medium bowl. Add the cinnamon, maple syrup, ¼ cup bourbon, butter, and brown sugar. Stir to combine.

8. Heat the apple mixture in a large skillet over medium-low heat. Cook until the apples are tender and the liquid has thickened, about 10 to 12 minutes. Mix the plain precooked and crumbled bacon into the apple filling. Set aside to cool.

9. Combine the heavy cream, powdered sugar, and 1 tablespoon bourbon in a large chilled bowl. Whip with a hand mixer until soft peaks are formed.

10. Use the tip of a small spoon to carefully remove a tiny circle of puff pastry from the center of each tart, creating a well. Fill each tart with 1 tablespoon of the apple filling.

11. Put the filled tarts on a serving platter. Top with a dollop of whipped cream and garnish with shards of the candied bacon.

BRIAN'S KITCHEN POINTER

You can make this dessert your own by choosing a different type of apple. Visit a local farmers' market or well-stocked grocery store and you'll find an amazing variety of apples, each with their own flavor. Avoid McIntosh and red delicious as they can get mushy or mealy when cooked. I buy organic because non-organic apples are usually treated with a lot of chemicals you don't need in your dessert.

CARAMEL BANANA CREAM PIE

I toured with Champions on Ice for over seventeen years. We had an all-star international cast that included a lot of spectacular Russian skaters. In the years before the Iron Curtain fell, my Russian friends really looked forward to coming to America. One of the things I remember most about those early years is that whenever fresh fruit—especially bananas—was set down in the dressing rooms, the Russian skaters ran to them. It made me realize that we American skaters always took for granted the abundance of fresh fruit available here.

Knowing how much the Russians loved fresh fruit, one of the American skaters' moms would make a banana cream pie and bring it to Pittsburgh when we traveled through. Besides that pie, I don't think I've ever had banana cream pie that actually had chunks of fresh bananas in the filling. I love banana cream pie anyway, but here is my version with fresh ripe bananas and caramel. For me, this is a great combination of flakey crust, gooey caramel sauce, tasty banana chunks, and creamy custard filling. Don't be intimidated by the number of steps to prepare this. It really isn't very complicated . . . and the payoff is worth it.

SERVES 8

PIE:

6 ounces vanilla wafers (about 45 cookies)

1 tablespoon packed brown sugar

6 tablespoons (¾ stick) unsalted butter, melted, plus 2 tablespoons cut into pieces and softened

1 vanilla bean

1½ cups whole milk

⅓ cup granulated sugar, divided

Pinch of salt

4 large egg yolks

¼ cup cornstarch, sifted

2 ripe bananas

1 tablespoon fresh lemon juice

¼ cup sweetened shredded coconut

1 cup heavy cream

2 tablespoons superfine sugar

1 teaspoon pure vanilla extract

CARAMEL SAUCE:

½ cup granulated sugar

½ teaspoon cream of tartar

⅓ cup heavy cream

1. Preheat the oven to 350°F.

2. Process the wafers and brown sugar in the bowl of a food processor fitted with the metal blade until finely ground. Add the melted butter and pulse 3 or 4 times, or just until the mixture sticks together. (Do not overblend, as you do not want the mixture to turn pasty. You should have very fine crumbs.)

3. Scrape the crumb mixture into a shallow 9-inch glass pie dish and press it uniformly across the bottom and up the sides. (Use the back of a large shallow spoon.)

4. Bake the crust for 6 to 8 minutes, or until the edges begin to turn golden. Remove and set aside to cool to room temperature. It will firm up as it cools.

5. Slice the vanilla bean in half lengthwise and scrape out the seeds. Combine the seeds, pod, milk, half the granulated sugar, and the salt in a medium saucepan. Bring to a simmer over medium heat, whisking to dissolve the sugar.

6. Remove the pan from the heat and let the mixture steep for 10 minutes. Remove and discard the vanilla bean pod.

7. Meanwhile, beat the egg yolks, cornstarch, and remaining half of the sugar in a large mixing bowl with a hand mixer on medium, until the mixture is thick and pale yellow, about 2 minutes. With the mixer on slow, add about $\frac{1}{2}$ cup of the warm milk mixture to the egg yolks and beat until smooth.

8. Pour the egg-milk mixture into the pan with the remaining milk and whisk vigorously to combine. Return the pan to the stove over medium-low heat for 5 to 7 minutes, whisking occasionally, until the custard thickens to the consistency of pudding.

9. Remove the pan from the heat and whisk in the softened butter pieces with forceful strokes to keep the custard smooth. Cover the custard with plastic wrap and refrigerate for at least 30 minutes, or until chilled.

10. To make the caramel sauce, combine the sugar and cream of tartar with $\frac{1}{4}$ cup of water in a small saucepan. Bring to a simmer over medium heat and simmer gently for 7 to 10 minutes, or until the caramel turns light amber.

11. Remove from the heat and slowly and steadily pour the cream into the caramel in a stream, whisking constantly. As you add the cream, it will bubble vigorously. Set the caramel aside to cool to room temperature.

12. After the custard has chilled, mash 1 banana and whisk it and the lemon juice into the custard until smooth.

13. Pour about three-quarters of the caramel sauce over the bottom of the piecrust. Cut the remaining banana into $\frac{1}{4}$-inch-thick slices and layer over the caramel. Pour the custard filling over the bananas. Cover the pie with plastic wrap and refrigerate while you prepare the topping.

14. Spread the coconut on a baking sheet and toast in the oven for 4 to 5 minutes, or until lightly browned. Remove and let the coconut cool completely.

15. In a large, chilled mixing bowl, beat the cream, superfine sugar, and vanilla with an electric hand mixer on medium-high speed until slightly stiff peaks form, about 2 to 4 minutes.

16. Spread the cream topping over the chilled pie. Drizzle the remaining caramel sauce over the topping, sprinkle with the toasted coconut, and serve.

BRIAN'S KITCHEN POINTER

Superfine sugar will dissolve more readily in cream than granulated sugar does. You can find superfine sugar in the baking aisle of any supermarket right next to the other sugars, or you can make your own by whirling granulated sugar in a food processor until it is finely ground.

FRESH BERRIES *with* DULCE *de* LECHE WHIPPED CREAM

Dulche de leche, literally translated, means "milk candy." It's basically sugar and milk fat and gets its taste from the caramelized sugar. It pairs well with fresh fruits in season or even out-of-season berries, which you can have year-round because they freeze so well. This is a light dessert that comes together easily. Try serving it at dinner parties for a light, sweet course. As far as desserts go, this one is pretty friendly to the waistline. You can always monitor how much of a dollop of cream you put on top.

SERVES 4

½ pint fresh raspberries

½ pint fresh blueberries

1 pint fresh strawberries, quartered

6 basil leaves, sliced thinly,
    plus 4 sprigs for garnish

1 cup heavy cream

¼ cup dulce de leche

1 teaspoon vanilla extract

1. Combine the berries and sliced basil in a large bowl and toss to mix together. Evenly distribute the berries between 4 wine glasses or small bowls.

2. Combine the heavy cream, dulce de leche, and vanilla in a large chilled metal bowl. Whip until soft peaks form, using a whisk or electric mixer.

3. Place a large dollop of the cream on top of the berries, garnish each with a basil sprig, and serve immediately.

BRIAN'S KITCHEN POINTER

You can usually find canned dulce de leche in the ethnic-food section of a grocery store. If not, it's easy enough to make your own. Place an unopened can of evaporated milk in a deep pot and cover with water. Boil the water for 2 to 3 hours, then let the can cool. When you open it, you'll find delicious, caramel-colored dulce de leche. Whether you buy it or make it, you can use any leftover dulce de leche as a topping for ice cream, in milk shakes, as a filling for crepes, or mixed into plain yogurt.

NECTARINE *and* ALMOND CROSTATAS

Want a super-fast dessert that will wow your dinner guests? Of course you do! Look no further. The filling for this version of a classic Italian dessert can be made and refrigerated up to two days in advance. The almond-paste crust is ultra easy because it's already made, so you can throw the dessert together in less than half an hour. And this dessert is also totally adaptable. Want to change up the flavor of the filling? Replace the cream cheese with mascarpone. Not a fan of nectarines? Go with the classic Italian choices of cherries, berries, apricots, or pears. Want a richer finish? Substitute whipped cream for the ice cream. There are so many ways to go with this dessert, and they are all good!

SERVES 8

1 (8-ounce) package cream cheese, softened

2 tablespoons granulated sugar

1 tablespoon all-purpose flour, plus more for dusting

2 eggs, divided

1 teaspoon vanilla extract

2 (7-ounce) packages almond paste

4 nectarines, peeled

2 tablespoons raw sugar

1 pint vanilla ice cream (optional)

¼ cup sliced almonds, toasted

8 fresh mint sprigs

1. Preheat the oven to 375°F. Line 2 baking sheets with parchment paper and set aside.

2. Combine the cream cheese, sugar, flour, 1 egg, and vanilla in a large chilled metal bowl. Beat with a hand mixer until well blended and smooth. Set aside.

3. Divide each package of almond paste into 4 equal portions. Dust a work surface with flour and roll each portion into a 6-inch round, about ⅛-inch thick.

4. Place 2 tablespoons of the cream cheese filling into the center of each round. Spread the filling out in an even layer, stopping about ½ inch from the edge of the round.

5. Cut each nectarine in half and remove the pits. Cut each half into 5 slices.

6. Fan out 5 of the nectarine slices on top of the filling in the center of a round. Gently fold the edges of the almond paste over the edge of the filling all the way around. Transfer to a baking sheet and repeat with the remaining ingredients, filling both sheets.

7. Whisk together the remaining egg and 1 tablespoon of water in a small bowl until well blended. Using a pastry brush, lightly brush each crostata with the egg wash and sprinkle with raw sugar.

8. Bake the crostatas until golden brown, about 20 minutes. Remove from the oven and let cool.

9. Serve each crostata on a plate with a small scoop of ice cream, if desired, and garnished with sliced almonds and mint.

PUDDING UPGRADES

My mom had a few signature dishes, and one of my all-time favorites was her very simple "Black and White Pie." She had a special oversize pie tin that she would line with a graham cracker crust and top with a layer of banana pudding, then a layer of chocolate pudding. She would then cover the pie with whipped cream. My brother, sisters, and I absolutely loved that pie, and we still talk about it. We'd race through dinner just to get to it.

I can't compete with Mom, so I came up with my own slant on pudding. The Horchata Rice Pudding on page 210 pays tribute to her famous pie. It's a slightly more elegant take on classic pudding and a great choice for a dinner party.

COCONUT FLAN

I made this flan for a party I threw for my friend Renee on my show. For that episode, I prepared a Cuban feast that included roasting a whole pig. Truth be told, the pork didn't come out so well. I really needed something to redeem myself, and this coconut flan saved the night! Never underestimate the power of simple flavors. A bit of sugar, a rich body, and a sprinkling of coconut all make for a killer meal-ender. It's just rich enough to top off a heavy meal, but not so much that people feel overly full. Bring it to the table uncut, with the caramel spilling over the sides, for an impressive presentation.

SERVES 8

1 cup granulated sugar

2 (13.5-ounce) cans coconut milk

1 (14-ounce) can sweetened condensed milk

3 large whole eggs

2 large egg yolks

Zest of 1 lime

¼ cup unsweetened flaked coconut

1. Preheat the oven to 325°F.

2. Combine the sugar with ¼ cup of water in a heavy saucepan over high heat. Stir and let simmer until the mixture reaches a deep amber color.

3. Pour the mixture into a 9-inch cake pan, swirling to completely coat the bottom. Set aside to cool and harden.

4. Combine the milks, eggs, and egg yolks in a blender and blend well. Add the lime zest and pulse 2 times to barely combine. Pour the blended mixture into the cake pan over the hardened caramel base.

5. Bake in a water bath until set (the center will still be slightly wobbly), about 1 hour. Remove and let cool completely before refrigerating for 2 hours.

6. Toast the flaked coconut in a large dry skillet over medium-low heat until light brown, stirring often. Remove from the heat and let cool.

7. Run a knife around the edge of the flan and invert it onto a large plate. Cut into slices, garnish with the toasted coconut, and serve.

HORCHATA RICE PUDDING

This is a great dessert for people who don't eat dairy because it's made with horchata instead of milk. Horchata is a traditional Spanish sweet drink made with ground almonds, sesame seeds, or rice and combined with sugar. It is often served with desserts such as Mexican churros. This creamy pudding has a firm consistency and interesting texture because of the chewy rice. The vanilla and nutmeg add another layer of nutty sweetness to the dish. People are often surprised to find rice pudding under a crème brûlée caramelized-sugar crust. That sugar crust gives it the added layer of sweet crunch.

SERVES 8

1 cup arborio rice, rinsed

½ cup granulated sugar

2½ cups almond milk

2½ cups rice milk

1 cinnamon stick

¼ teaspoon freshly ground nutmeg

1 vanilla bean

¼ cup turbinado sugar (recommended: Sugar in the Raw)

1. Combine the rice, granulated sugar, milks, cinnamon stick, and nutmeg in a large saucepan. Split the vanilla bean, scrape the seeds from the pod, and add both to the saucepan.

2. Simmer over low heat until the rice turns soft, with a thick, pudding-like consistency, about 30 to 40 minutes. (Be careful not to bring the rice to a full boil.)

3. Remove the cinnamon stick and vanilla bean pod. Divide the mixture between 8 ramekins and refrigerate until completely cool.

4. Sprinkle turbinado sugar over the top of each ramekin. Caramelize the sugar with a kitchen torch until golden brown. If you do not have a blowtorch, arrange the ramekins on a sheet pan and put under a broiler until the sugar has caramelized, about 5 to 7 seconds.

BRIAN'S KITCHEN POINTER

Treat your sweet tooth to a whole new experience with turbinado sugar. Also known as raw sugar, the coarse, light brown crystals are unrefined, so the flavor is more complex than processed white cane sugar. Turbinado includes hints of molasses and plenty of satisfying crunch, making it ideal for desserts such as the Horchata Rice Pudding here, crème brûlée, baked tarts, or even pancakes. And it's great for flashy dinner party presentations; a sprinkle of this sugar over the top of your favorite dessert can literally make it sparkle!

MENUS

IF YOU'VE READ THIS FAR, YOU KNOW THAT THE RECIPES in this cookbook range far and wide. I like a lot of variety in my cooking, combining an eclectic new mix from my travels with old favorites. It's like having a lot of options in my playbook. I like to have recipes ready for any particular occasion, season, or whim I might have. If you're like me, you have a group of recipes—what I call "The Regulars"—that you go to again and again. And then you have other more adventurous dishes for when you want to try something a little bit different. The trick is to make the most of any recipes you choose by combining them into winning meals. Making a memorable menu is part art and part science, but it's the key to creating special-occasion meals—no matter what the occasion is.

I know that process can be a bit of a mystery to the home cook. Ideally, you want your meal to "present" well even if it is a simple affair like an informal weekend brunch. The dishes should look good together, contain flavors that complement one another, and have the right "scale"—you don't want to leave your guests (or yourself) hungry, but you also don't want people feeling stuffed. Feel free to experiment with different combinations; it's part of cooking creatively. I have some friends who love to have people over for dinner parties, but their schedules are so busy that they don't have the time to sit down and figure out the menu. If you are like them, you can turn to the ready-made menus I've provided for you in this chapter. I won't tell.

BRUNCH

Smoked Salmon with Lemon Crème Fraîche and Capers, page 18

Sautéed Vegetable, Chicken, and Quinoa Salad, page 64

Fresh Berries with Dulce de Leche Whipped Cream, page 204

Ham, Brie, and Apple Butter Panini, page 46

Napa Cabbage with Ginger and Sesame Oil Stir-Fry, page 170

Horchata Rice Pudding, page 210

HEARTY LUNCH

Grilled Cheese Sandwich with Red Onion Jam, page 48

Sweet Corn Chowder, page 58

Spicy Coffee Brownies, page 196

LIGHTER LUNCH

Sun-Dried Tomato Chicken Salad, page 68

Spicy Sausage Soup with Cannellini Beans and Escarole, 56

Coconut Flan, page 209

CASUAL DINNERS

Missed Putt Pizza, page 50

Carrot and Red Cabbage Slaw with Creamy Herb Dressing, page 76

Nectarine and Almond Crostatas, page 206

Not Your Mama's Spaghetti and Meatballs, page 104

Spicy Snap Peas (Italian style), page 172

Caramel Banana Cream Pie, page 202

Cucumber and Radish Salad, page 78

Spice-Rubbed Brick Cornish Game Hens, page 140

Rigatoni with Spicy Chicken Sausage, Asparagus, Eggplant, and Roasted Peppers
(vegetarian version), page 102

HEARTY DINNERS

Braised Hawaiian Pork Shoulder, page 124

Mashed Parsnips and Celery Root, page 167

Tartufo, page 188

Butternut Squash Soup with Goat Cheese Toasts, page 54

Short Rib Bourguignon, page 118

Roasted Winter Vegetables, page 182

Horchata Rice Pudding, page 210

ELEGANT COMFORT

Polenta with Spicy Sausage and Red Pepper Relish, page 8

Rosemary Braised Lamb Shanks, page 131

Olive-and-Herb Red Potatoes, page 175

Bourbon Bacon Apple Tarts, page 199

White Bean, Caramelized Onion, and Artichoke Bruschetta, page 6

Shrimp and Polenta, page 152

Chocolate Almond Panna Cotta, page 194

CLASSIC DINNERS

Heirloom Tomato, Cantaloupe, and Feta Salad, page 75

Pan-Roasted Filet Mignon with Balsamic Syrup and Asparagus, page 113

Olive-and-Herb Red Potatoes, page 175

Molten Chocolate Cakes with Raspberry Sauce, page 191

Arugula and Nectarine Salad with Pepperoncini Vinaigrette and Olive Bread Croutons, page 71

Coq au Vin-guine, page 100

Spicy Coffee Brownies, page 196

SPECIAL OCCASION

Sun-Dried Tomato and Goat Cheese Skewers, page 16
Sea Bass with Roasted Cauliflower Puree and Leek Buerre Blanc, page 160
Nectarine and Almond Crostatas, page 206

Crispy Crab Cakes with Avocado-Citrus Salad, page 146
Grilled Rack of Lamb with Red Chimichurri Sauce, page 128
Butternut Squash and Goat Cheese Gratin, page 176
Molten Chocolate Cakes with Raspberry Sauce, page 191

QUICK WEEKNIGHT MEALS

Penne with Broccoli Rabe and Goat Cheese, page 92
Fresh Berries with Dulce de Leche Whipped Cream, page 204

Spaghetti Carbonara, page 98
Spicy Snap Peas (Italian style), page 172
Tartufo, page 188

Thai Red Curry Chicken, page 138
Napa Cabbage with Ginger and Sesame Oil Stir-Fry, page 170

COOL COCKTAIL PARTIES

When I think of cocktail parties, I think of Tom Collins—not the drink, the man. Tom was the producer of Champions on Ice, and I traveled with that show for twenty-five tours over seventeen years. Once a year at the U.S. Figure Skating Championships, Tommy would throw the be-all and end-all of cocktail parties. It was the highlight of the week for judges, skaters, coaches, and parents. I usually intended to leave early, but the food was over the top and the cocktails were flowing. Instead I always closed down that party—sometimes literally the last one to leave. Now that's a great cocktail party, when you don't want it to end!

Crispy Crab Cakes with Avocado-Citrus Salad, page 146
Hot Italian Sausage Panini with Pickled Peppers, page 44
Beef Satay, page 12
Marky DV, page 33
Passion Fruit and Mango Mar-Tony, page 38

Paella Sliders, page 4
Southwestern Sopapillas, page 10
Polenta with Spicy Sausage and Red Pepper Relish, page 8
Carne Asada Tacos with Green Salsa, page 110
Selection of Beers and Tequila

Parmesan-Crusted Brussels Sprouts, page 180
Ham, Brie, and Apple Butter Panini, page 46
Sun-Dried Tomato Chicken Salad, page 68
Spicy Coffee Brownies, page 196
The Calhoun, page 32
Lemon Meringue, page 34

GLOSSARY

AL DENTE: An Italian term that literally translates to "to the tooth," and describes perfectly done pasta that has a very slight snap or resistance when bitten. Lack of this firmness is a sign of overdone pasta.

BÉCHAMEL: This is a simple, useful sauce made from a roux base of butter and flour, to which milk is added. Bland and thin, béchamel is often used as the base for other sauces.

BLANCH: A cooking process that preserves the vitamins, crunch, and color of vegetables by cooking the vegetables in boiling water for a short time, then immediately placing them into an ice bath to stop the cooking process.

BOUQUET GARNI: A "bouquet" of fresh herbs tied with the green part of a scallion or leek, or placed in a cheesecloth bag, and added to soups, sauces, stews, or poaching liquids to add intense herbal flavors.

BRAISE: The process of cooking pork, chicken, or meat for long periods in liquid at low heat. Braised dishes are often browned first to start the cooking process, and the braising liquid is used as a base for brown sauces or gravy.

BRINE: The term used for both heavily salted water and the process of soaking food in that water to cure it or keep it tender and juicy during cooking.

BROIL: Cooking food directly under or directly above an intense heat source.

BRUSCHETTA: This Italian term means "to roast over coals," referring to the toasted bread that serves as the base for most bruschetta, over which is laid any of a vast number of toppings to create wonderful finger food or appetizers.

BUTTERFLY: The technique of splitting fowl, fish, and even certain cuts of meat down the center, so that the flesh is more exposed to the cooking surface.

CANOLA OIL: A relatively heart-healthy cooking oil made from rapeseed. It's less distinctively flavored than olive oil, making it ideal for dishes cooked in oil where you want the flavors of the food to stand out and not be affected by the flavor of the oil.

CHIFFONADE: A French term that means to cut or slice into thin strips.

CHILE PASTE: Made from crushed chiles, vinegar, and other spices, chile paste is a great way to saturate a dish with the essence of the chile (and is also easier to handle than many hot chiles). You'll find the paste in mild, medium, and hot versions.

CHORIZO: Sausage made with a distinctive blend of hot spices. Mexican-style chorizo is made with fresh pork; Spanish-style is made with smoked pork and tastes noticeably different.

CRÈME FRAÎCHE: A richer version of sour cream, with the same consistency but a slightly tangier, fuller-bodied flavor.

CUT IN: The process of mixing shortening such as lard or butter into dry ingredients. This is traditionally done with a pastry blender, although you can use your fingers, a stand blender, or a food processor, depending on the recipe.

DEGLAZE: Freeing the remnants that are stuck to the pan after sautéing. Deglazing is done with a liquid, most often a cooking alcohol such as Madeira or cooking sherry. The liquid formed from deglazing is usually used as the foundation for a sauce.

DEGORGE: The process of removing moisture from certain foods by sprinkling them with salt, and then patting dry once the water has sweated out of the food. This is also the term used to describe removing sand from shellfish by adding cornmeal to soaking water.

DE-VEIN: Removing the black vein from the spine of a shrimp. The vein is cut out with a sharp knife run down the outside curve of raw shrimp. The vein is removed because it can negatively impact flavor.

DOCK: Puncturing a crust before baking to allow steam to escape and prevent the crust from puffing up. This can be done with a fork or a special tool called a "docker."

DOUBLE BOILER: A set of pots, one sitting atop and slightly inside the other. Double boilers are used to melt materials that might overreact to direct heat, such as chocolate and cream. You can create your own double boiler using the same principle of boiling water in a chamber below any pot. Also known as a bain-marie.

DREDGE: The technique of evenly coating foods for frying. It can involve breading with an egg mixture and bread crumbs or cornmeal, or other versions such as coating food in batter.

DRY RUB: A blend of spices used in place of a marinade to tenderize and flavor meat or fowl.

EMULSIFY: The process of combining two liquids that normally would not be mixed, such as water and oil. It is done by slowly adding one to the other while whisking or mixing vigorously. Vinaigrette is a typical example of an emulsion.

FOLD: Combining a light mix of ingredients into a heavy mix of ingredients, as with the liquid combination that is mixed into the dry ingredients in a cake recipe. Folding is as much the technique as the process, which is usually done with a flat tool such as a spatula, "cutting" the top ingredients into the bottom ingredients.

FLUTING: The technique of crimping the edge of pastry or dough, either with a fork, a special tool, or by hand. It is used to enclose pastry shells for dishes from pies to empanadas.

GANACHE: A simple blend of cream and chocolate mixed over low heat. The texture, taste, and stiffness are controlled by altering the amounts of chocolate or cream. Ganache is an extremely useful dessert component, one that can serve as icing or filling, or be used alone as truffles.

INFUSE: Steeping a flavorful aromatic ingredient in a hot liquid, so that the ingredient intensely flavors the liquid. Although tea is the most common infusion, the process can be used to flavor all kinds of desserts, sauces, and other liquids.

JULIENNE: To cut vegetables into thin, uniform slices (although any food can technically be julienned). Maintaining uniformity is difficult when julienning by hand, which is why food is usually julienned with a mandoline slicer.

MACERATE: The process of soaking foods in a liquid to give the food the flavor of the liquid. This is most often done with liqueurs and other alcohols, although simple syrup is sometimes used.

MULL: To add spices and sweeteners to a beverage, and then slowly warm it so that the flavors mix and saturate the beverage.

PARBOIL: See Blanch.

PARE: To use a knife or peeler to remove the skin or top layer of a fruit or vegetable.

PHYLLO DOUGH: This is amazingly convenient prepared dough sold in sheets. The dough bakes into a flaky pastry that can be used in all kinds of dishes, and is a lot easier than making pastry shells or crusts from scratch.

PROOF: The process of letting dough rise by allowing it to sit for several hours, undisturbed, in a warm, humid place (or under a towel).

QUENCH: See Blanch.

QUESO BLANCO: Crumbly, mild Mexican white cheese that originated in Spain. Queso blanco is the Mexican version of mozzarella, and is just as adaptable in recipes. It complements salads and traditional Mexican dishes, and even works as topping for stews.

RECONSTITUTE: To return a dried food or condensed liquid to its original form and volume by adding water.

REDUCE: To thicken and decrease the volume of a liquid with high heat, a process that intensifies flavors and creates sauces with a thicker body.

ROUX: A base formed of butter and flour. A roux is generally used as a foundation for sauces, browned for brown sauces and left white for white sauces.

SAUTÉ: From the French "to jump," sautéing is simply the process of cooking food quickly in preheated, hot fat such as butter or oil. Done correctly, sautéing seals in juices and flavor without giving the food an opportunity to soak up too much of the fat.

SCALD: A commonly misunderstood term that means to heat liquid to just below boiling, so that bubbles form around the edges of the liquid. Milk is the liquid most often scalded, and care must be taken not to burn the liquid or the burnt taste will permeate it. This term is sometimes used in place of "blanch" when the goal is to move a fruit or vegetable from boiling water to an ice bath in order to remove the skin of the fruit or vegetable.

SCALLOP: A preparation technique in which the food is sliced thin and layered, then cooked in a casserole dish, often topped with cheese or bread crumbs.

SCORE: To cut slits on the surface of food. The slits can be used to release steam, absorb flavor from a cooking liquid, or allow fats to drain from the food during cooking.

SEAR: Another commonly misunderstood term, sear means to quickly brown the surface of meat, poultry, or fish so that juices are sealed in and an appealing crispy texture is created on the surface. Food can be seared in a pan or under a broiler.

SHUCK: To remove the husks from corn or the shells from seafood.

TRUSS: To wrap food, usually meat or poultry, with twine or scallion or leek stems. The technique holds food together when combined in a roll or cooked to extreme tenderness, such as in braising.

VELOUTÉ: Sauce that is a variation on béchamel, with chicken, fish, or vegetable stock replacing the milk.

WEEP: The process of water drawing out of food. This can happen by dusting the food with salt, or as a food is warmed, such as with custard.

ZEST: The action, and material produced, of removing the outer layer of any citrus fruit with a grater or other instrument. Zesting must be done carefully so that only the flavorful, colored outer layer is removed and the bitter, white "pith" is left intact.

INDEX

ACKNOWLEDGMENTS

Thank you Chris Peterson for keeping me on track, staying organized, and suggesting adjectives to take the place of the dreaded "flavorful" word (I did say it sometimes). You inspired me to add more of myself and recount great memories in my life that I had almost forgotten.

Lara Asher. Thank you for backing me from the beginning and sharing your helpful insight and suggestions. Your guidance and enthusiasm have always been encouraging. And you make a dang good recipe tester.

Thank you to my book agents Jane Dystel and Miriam Goderich for your hard work, persistence, and belief in this book.

Tim Macklin you are invaluable and tireless. It's such a pleasure to share my food life with you. You are one of the reasons I like food even more . . . and that's almost impossible. You are the best bar none.

Rina Jordan. Your photos are delicious, beautiful, and they make me very hungry. Thank you for working under the gun and often long distance.

Malina Lopez—food stylist goddess. You never failed to deliver sumptuous food and setups. I still want the bowl on page 75.

Franc, thank you for being my recipe guinea pig and never complaining when a dish was smoky or when I accidently added cilantro—the two things you dislike most.

Linda, I can only say WOW. Thank you for decades of quality control and inspiration in every aspect of my career. I couldn't do it without you, and I'm so lucky to have you watching my back. From falling on two-foot spins to a cookbook—it's been a crazy good ride.

To my family, for inspiring me to continue the old family traditions and make new ones.

And finally, mom and dad. Thank you for providing an endless amount of fantastic and loving memories that I can share with people. I've said it before and I will say it again, you are the poster parents for unconditional love and support.

ABOUT THE AUTHOR

Brian Boitano is more than just a champion on the ice; he also gives a winning performance in the kitchen. His Food Network series, *What Would Brian Boitano Make?*, premiered in August 2009 and is now on the Cooking Channel. On the air, Brian demonstrates his culinary skills and talent for one-of-a-kind entertaining. With a lifelong passion for food and cooking, Brian hosts unpredictable get-togethers at his San Francisco home and creates menus that focus on innovative but accessible dishes.

Few athletes have enjoyed the artistic and popular success that Brian has since winning the gold medal for the United States at the 1988 Winter Olympics Games in Calgary, Canada. He created and routinely performs his signature jump, the Tano Triple, so difficult it has rarely been completed by anyone else. In competitions and exhibitions, Brian continues to raise the level of skating to new heights. After turning professional in 1988, he won six world professional titles, placing first and scoring perfect 10s in each of ten consecutive championships. As a professional, he won the first twenty out of the twenty-four competitions he entered, a record unmatched in the history of skating. Brian has won more professional titles than any other skater in the history of the sport; among those titles are six World Professional Championships.

Brian won a primetime Emmy Award, television's highest honor, for his starring role in the 1990 HBO movie *Carmen on Ice*. In 1992 he and fellow Olympic gold medalist Katarina Witt toured North America in three successful ice shows: *Skating, Skating II*, and *Skating '92,* which were broadcast on network television. In 1994 he starred in *Nutcracker on Ice* with Oksana Baiul and Viktor Petrenko. For fifteen years he toured with Champions on Ice around the country, headlining twenty-five national tours. Brian has provided expert commentary on televised skating shows for ABC, NBC, and Turner networks.

Brian is a three-time Olympian and has won more than fifty titles, including twenty-three international gold medals, two World titles, two Pro/AM titles, sixteen professional titles, and four U.S. National titles, as well as the Olympic Gold Medal. He has been inducted into the World Figure Skating Hall of Fame, the U.S. Figure Skating Hall of Fame, and the National Italian-American Hall of Fame. In 1998 Brian founded Youth Skate, a nonprofit organization that introduces San Francisco's inner-city youth to the sport of ice skating. He lives in the San Francisco Bay area.